BECAUSE
OF
BRETT

BECAUSE
OF
BRETT

Sarah Woodier

The Book Guild Ltd

First published in Great Britain in 2021 by
The Book Guild Ltd
9 Priory Business Park
Wistow Road, Kibworth
Leicestershire, LE8 0RX
Freephone: 0800 999 2982
www.bookguild.co.uk
Email: info@bookguild.co.uk
Twitter: @bookguild

Typeset in 11pt Minion Pro

Printed and bound by CPI Group (UK) Ltd, Croydon, CR0 4YY

ISBN 978 1913551 643

British Library Cataloguing in Publication Data.
A catalogue record for this book is available from the British Library.

This book is dedicated to the babies, children and teenagers we were honoured to meet along Brett's cancer path, who also lost their lives.

Jay Demetriou
Chelsea Street
Ben Parkhouse
Joel Smith
Jordan Berridge
Sian Nokes
Jamie Cartwright
Jordan Cobby
Laura Rowley
Taro Moore
Ross Emslie
Lauryn Lee
Shayne Hartley
Ronnie Manders
Rajan, Niamh, Harry and Jessica.
And of course, our hero, Brett Woodier.

I know I will have left many names off this list so please accept my apologises in advance, it just that there were so many and I misplaced my original list.

Chapter 1

My Legend's Story

Zombies are real. They live on our streets and they walk amongst us every day. These creatures are extremely lifelike, as they look just like any normal human being, but they are not like us; these creatures are very different because they are devoid of all the normal standard human emotions. The zombies' emotions are erratic and extremely unpredictable, as they range from states of haunted emptiness, unfeeling and cold, to, in contrast, explosions of excessive episodes of rage and anger like never seen before over the seemingly most trivial things.

These zombies are cold, unfeeling and appear unloving. They show no emotion when present during happy times such as weddings, birthdays or Christmas, and they do not care if you've just got a new puppy, kitten,

1

child or husband. They look like dead souls inhabiting a live human body, often seeming preoccupied, agitated and rarely peaceful.

Whilst these zombies physically dwell in this world, they mostly exist in another world which is in their own heads. You cannot leave your home without interacting with one of these zombies. Chances are we may ourselves become one of these zombies at some point in our lives and some of us may even stay in that zombie state forever. For these zombies are the grieving, the sad and the hurting who are struggling to function and remember how to behave 'normal' in a world that appears equally as cold and unforgiving as they themselves do.

Benjamin Franklin is quoted as saying: "In this world nothing can be said to be certain except death and taxes."

It's a good quote but not quite valid in this day and age, as a lot of big corporations and many rich people seem to be able to squirm their way out of paying taxes, so that just leaves death as the only certainty. But if that's correct, then why is the subject of death so shunned in modern society? You are far more welcome to discuss all the other well-known taboo subjects like sex, religion and politics than you are death.

Nowadays people generally seem to show more compassion and consideration for a famous person who's died than for their own friends and family. I suppose it's much easier to pour out emotions over Facebook about a person you've never met than it is to talk to the family of Uncle Sid who's not long passed. Although, those three words form the basis of the thread that drives me insane, 'not long passed'.

From the moment the person takes their last breath the clock starts ticking for the grieving family. The time limit on grieving is getting smaller and smaller; the window allowed to let the sadness in is minuscule. Grief, like any other unpleasant feeling in our society, must be eradicated, so one must hurry up and get over it.

"Move on, move on, move on," society cries. "It's what [he/she, or insert dead person's name] would have wanted."

"Life's too short to be sad; anyway, [he/she, or insert name again] had a good innings."

Blessed are the grieving, says the Bible. Well, that's certainly not the sentiment shared with the people of this fast-paced world. In today's society, funerals are organised with lightning speed, condolences are said over social media and if you haven't got over a death within two weeks then you need to see a doctor to get antidepressants or therapy, or both.

If anyone actually does get caught up in grief and takes their time with it (or it with them, as is often the case), they are either denounced as mentally ill or seen to be wallowing for attention. One gets medicated and the other gets scolded or ignored.

In our rigid modern societies, it seems as though we are not only told how to live our lives, including how we are allowed to die, but also, then, how we should grieve the dead. For everything there is a protocol to follow, a set of guidelines to adhere to – God forbid we should actually think or feel for ourselves independently.

Allegedly there are five, seven or twelve stages of grief (it depends on whose set of guidelines you're reading), but it's fair to say they are all pretty similar. The main five stages of grief are based on work by Elisabeth Kubler-Ross MD. She wrote a book in 1969 called *On Death and Dying* which was about her work with people who were terminally ill. The now-famous five stages she talked about in her book were her observations of the range of emotions a person who was dying would experience prior to their own death.

The stages she wrote about were: denial, anger, bargaining, depression and acceptance. People wishing to appear authoritative on the subject have since added on other stages, such as: shock, testing, numb, sadness, anxiety, fear and guilt, etc.

I am rolling my eyes and whispering, "No shit, Sherlock," even when typing these so-called stages due to their so very obvious nature. I almost feel like adding, "You might even cry."

To be clear, though, the original five stages were not actually about the grieving families and their emotions around those dying people, but instead about the dying individual themselves. Some genius somewhere obviously decided that these five stages she spoke of in her book, basic and obvious as they are, should form the basis of the generic instruction guide that is now robotically spewed out to all bereaved people.

Kubler-Ross herself repeatedly tried to denounce the constant references to her book and the overused five stages, and it was written in her later book with David Kessler, *On Grief and Grieving*:

"The stages have evolved since their introduction and they have been very misunderstood over the past three decades. They were never meant to help tuck messy emotions into neat packages. They are responses to loss that many people have, but there is not a typical response to loss, as there is no typical loss. Our grief is as individual as our lives."

The problem is society wants grief to be quantifiable. It's as if grief should be more organised, neat and tidy: "Just go through each of the five stages quoted and when you're finished you will have got to the other happy side and you will have officially been classified as 'moved on.'"

Some deaths, I suppose, maybe are quite neat and tidy; they might seem logical and even kind, especially after long illnesses. This book is about those deaths that are harder to accept, those painful losses that are not going to be easily soothed with a pamphlet about grief containing a clichéd, old and worn-out rationale.

Grief is not a one-size-fits-all event; it is life-changing and affects different people in different ways, and, I'm very sad to say, a lot of those ways are quite awful and rarely quick.

Now, I'm not trying to be a scare-monger or some voice of doom who's saying grief will destroy you – no, not at all; in fact, quite the contrary. We all know the only truth you can speak is your own, otherwise you risk repeating someone else's lies, and my truth is that the one-size-fits-all model on grieving is just rubbish. We've got to start talking openly about death in our society, as well as about those people whom we've lost personally. We have to take the 'death taboo' away.

Doctors say they know grief is so powerful; it can affect the physical body in a whole host of different ways with mysterious illnesses, aches and pains materialising only to magically disappear again in time. You can actually die of a broken heart; it's called 'takotsubo cardiomyopathy' or heartbreak syndrome. There is a mystique to grieving that doctors are trying to understand, but I don't think science is ever going to be able to manage it.

There's no doubt that the effects of losing someone you love is beyond what you have ever experienced before – beyond words, beyond pain, it's just so massive. Society dishing out a one-size-fits-all standard guide to what you're going to feel and experience is patronising at best and insulting at worst. Suggesting that these huge, emotional responses to losing our loved ones can be so basically categorised and standardised is belittling and infuriating.

I have a very different attitude and approach to grieving the people I have lost. I keep them with me. I refuse to move on. For me it's impossible and actually disgusting to suggest we discard the people we love who have died and just get on with our lives as though they never existed.

I say, "Bring out your dead and I will bring out mine!"

Figuratively speaking that is, and yes, it brings up weird imagery. (The fourteenth-century term 'bring out your dead' was shouted as the cart collecting those who had died of the bubonic plague passed by so you could throw your dead housemates on the cart for disposal.)

I personally rejoice at the realisation that I will never get over the death of my son and I refuse to even try. It doesn't mean that I haven't gone through those emotions mentioned in the stages and many more besides them as well. Actually, I'd say those emotions went through me is a more truthful account. But I refuse to believe I will ever be 'done' or 'finished' and 'over it', and I don't want to be! I love him, and I love loving him.

I no longer see grieving my son as suffering but more as it being just a part of who I am now. I love him so much. I feel calm to miss him freely. If I want to cry, I will; if I want to feel sad, I do; but I have no need, desire or expectation to be over it.

I feel my son around me at times; I see signs from him and I talk to him every day, and when I close my eyes and think of him, I feel a strong sense of love. That love connection never dies; it remains and it binds us together and holds us fast and tight. That love will carry me on until my last day.

I refuse to move on without my son, so instead I take him with me everywhere. I named my shop after him; this book has his name; I have his stuff everywhere still; a towel with the name Brett embroidered on it is in our family bathroom. He is included in everything – dinner reservations, invitations – and his name is always on cards and presents. It is forever going to be the four of us, even though one is only there in 'spirit', so to speak. It is the only way I have been able to cope with the gaping hole inside that's been left since he died. My love for him is so deep, I would have much rather died than him, but I wasn't allowed to swap places with him; it's not like I had the choice.

So, I encourage and cry out to the whole world:

> "Bring out your dead and I, too,
> will bring out mine!"

That is ultimately the message of my book. We need to share and talk and laugh and cry about our dead loved ones. Not in a morbid, cold way, but in a bright, warm and loving way.

Love never dies, energy never dies and our loved ones' souls are that eternal energy. They are with us still and if we would just stop for a minute and be very honest, we would confirm that on some level we know this to be true. Our loved ones are always with us.

Sadly, though, this energetic relationship often just isn't enough and that's what makes us all so sad.

Society encourages us to almost bury the very true essence of our loved ones, as well as their physical bodies, when they pass on. We are not encouraged to talk about our dead loved ones and if we ever do, we are only met with very uncomfortable silences, accompanied by awkward sideways glances by people who are openly squirming in their chairs. Should we continue to talk too much about our dead loved ones we are almost always cast as mentally ill and are positively encouraged to seek medical advice.

It's all utter nonsense. Why do we have to stop talking about our loved ones? It's crazy to think we should or even could stop thinking and talking about them.

In this cold, antisocial, social media-filled world, it is a miserable existence for anyone suffering loss and most of us will suffer one day or are maybe suffering right now. There is no longer a community around us; people are more spread out. Our friends and family can be in different towns and even countries, but even if they are close physically, people generally don't like talking about death, as it's a buzzkill and a downer.

The world around me when Brett died seemed a place full of bad advice, shock and devastation, wrapped in fair weather mottos, standardised comments and worn-out clichés.

I soon realised the world outside of me was futile and useless to help me, so I went within. I used meditation and mindfulness (and sometimes cider).

I desperately needed to quieten all the voices in my head whilst trying to remain courteous to the world around me (often failing badly on that one). I had no words to offer anyone; I felt silent. I felt cold on a level no one would understand unless they had felt it too. I was still and frozen, yet in screaming pain; I needed people so badly yet they repulsed me, so I pushed them away. I was a sea of contradictions and I remain that way still to this day.

I am aware that I am broken in comparison to the mass majority of society. I have a huge black hole where my beliefs used to be and there's absolutely no doubt that I am changed beyond measure. But I am comforted by the belief that our loved ones live on after death; in fact, I'm pretty sure of it. Brett is still around, somewhere.

For the record, I am not in denial; I know my son's body is dead. His ashes are in a box in the room where I type this. I am only too aware that the game we played and the fun we had whilst on this Earth together, is over.

The only thing that really mattered to me after Brett died was to make sure Poppy (his younger sister) was functioning and that she would continue coping in this world, especially now she was an only child with no other siblings.

I never wanted an only child; I also never wanted to watch my child slowly die over many years, but you just don't get a choice over your life's direction sometimes.

I was not under any illusions about the experience of grief prior to Brett's death, but I was, and sometimes still am, confused how I could be adrift in a sea of pain without any meaningful guidance. 'Get over it and move on' just was never going to wash with me.

I refuse to get over him – it's impossible, anyway – so I just live with it. I live with the pain. The constant 'missing' feeling becomes the new normal feeling. Grief doesn't kill you; it just feels like it sometimes.

But my message is this: you are strong enough and you will cope. You might not want to hear that, but it's true. For some reason we are fed this constant stream of how we are not good enough or strong enough, that we're all actually weak, broken or need fixing. It's just not true. We are all, without exception, very powerful individuals.

The death of a loved one won't kill you. Yes, you'll feel like shit, strongly in the beginning and, depending on your connection to the deceased, maybe forever. But you're still alive and kicking, so now what? How do you live on?

For me, it is to honour Brett's memory. I talk about him whenever I want, no matter how uncomfortable it makes people around me feel, and I keep him with me.

For me, he may not physically walk on this Earth with me until I die, but he will walk with me in my heart and mind constantly; I sometimes imagine him next to me. That's how I am able to live on. You do what you need to do; you do what soothes you and ignore what 'they' say, if they disagree.

People should be free to grieve however they want to and for however long they want to. Do what you need to do and act in a way that gives you comfort. I find it repulsive that to many people that grieving could be classed as a mental illness. I'm sad, not sick. Why do we allow this one-size-fits-all society? We need to stop being sheep and mindlessly following the herd. Tell me about your deceased loved ones and I will tell you about mine.

Who were they? What did they like? What did they dislike? What made them laugh?

Tell me your funny stories and be free to experience and revel in your memories of them. They did exist and they walked this Earth, and whilst you continue walking this Earth they can too, by your side in your heart and mind.

But here's the deal, here's the point I'm trying to make: talk about them only if you want to. It's your path, it's your loss, it's your choice – do it your way.

Brett's Story – How Did I Get Here?

14th September 2008

Our life, as we knew it, was over. 'Change' had just happened in an instant and it was vile.

Why couldn't I have had the lottery-win type of instant change? That also would have been change in an instant, but that would have been exciting. The chance of living a luxurious life with no financial worries would open the mind to an endless stream of options and possibilities and evoke feelings of safety, joy, fun and happiness. Why couldn't I have had that one?

We had been in the hospital a few days. Brett had started vomiting at home then suddenly turned yellow; he had been diagnosed with hepatitis of the liver, but no one knew why a healthy thirteen-year-old boy would get it. The team of doctors had conducted a series of tests and a few days later, when the doctor arrived asking if I would come for a chat, I had a bad feeling come over me. When the nurses were evicted from the staff room (some eating their lunch) so we could talk in private, my heart started racing. In the instant I was told my son had leukaemia, I experienced something that felt like I was physically falling, then my mind went blank. I even said, "Isn't leukaemia cancer?", which I already knew it was. I couldn't take on board anything the doctor was saying; I only heard vague mumblings.

Then came the tears, but I decided to hide them from my son. I didn't want to tell him he had cancer whilst blubbering all over him; I wanted to show him my strength and determination that we would get through this. After I was told the awful news, I went straight outside the hospital and phoned my husband, even though the doctors had just told me not to.

My son had been in hospital for over a week and my husband and I had started to do twenty-four-hour 'shifts' due to the travelling to and from the hospital; it also enabled us to take care of our younger daughter. I phoned him at home to give him time to digest the news, cry and toughen up ready for later. My husband has always agreed he would have done the same thing. Doctors follow protocols based on case studies and research – I know my own partner, thank you very much.

Telling my son of his diagnosis was the hardest thing I had ever done and remains indescribably painful, and yes, even with my best intentions I did cry; we all did.

A few days into our cancer hell the consultant took my husband and I into a side room to 'sign some forms'. I thought it was weird, as he wanted us both there at the same time and yet we had both signed different consent forms and only one signature was normally needed. *Hey ho*, I thought. *They know what they're doing.*

What he actually wanted was to tell us alone, away from Brett, that Brett would die within a few days if they didn't treat him and would die instantly if they did start treatment. His liver and body were so toxic that the normal chemotherapy dose would kill him outright.

I remember shooting a quick glance at my husband and looking straight back at the doctor as he sat in silence. I was waiting for the 'but' – there had to be a 'but' – and after what seemed like an age, the 'but' came. He could only offer an experiment, an educated guess, and there was no prognosis for our son and definitely no promises.

The guess experiment involved putting small levels of chemotherapy into his body with the hope that it would help his liver heal. The combination of the hepatitis and leukaemia meant his body's toxicity levels were too high to treat normally.

The chances were slim at best, but it was worth a try – what did we think? As if he had to ask.

Yes, yes, yes, we said.

I realised an experiment was not good and the outcome was extremely shaky, but it gave us hope, and once you've got some hope you can start to pick up – hope is everything.

I remember coming out of the room smiling, not sad. I was not an idiot and I knew my son was dangerously ill; he had been for ten days at that point. It was a relief to finally know what was wrong with him and that the doctors had a plan, albeit a very scary one.

I had hope, and that felt so amazing after all the dark fear and panic. Hope was a good feeling.

***

My son Brett was diagnosed with acute lymphoblastic leukaemia presenting in the liver (which is rare) in September 2008; he was thirteen years old. The experiment worked and Brett's liver responded very well. He was on full 'normal' treatment by the December.

A very long and torturous battle ensued until he was happily given the all-clear in September 2011 and allowed to stop chemotherapy. He had suffered so much, as his body was seemingly sensitive to every element of the disgusting treatment.

The happiness was short-lived, as Brett's leukaemia relapsed ten months later in June 2012; his only hope now would be a bone marrow transplant.

After an extensive worldwide search, a donor was thankfully found and he had his bone marrow transplant in November 2012; he was in hospital over Christmas 2012 and came out just a few days before his eighteenth birthday in January 2013.

Sadly, his body never really recovered from the transplant, and although he was cancer-free, his health never improved. He was given a top-up of the donor cells the following September 2013. He spent the last year of his life still in isolation and in and out of the hospital until eventually he was in multi-organ failure led by his liver and kidneys.

The treatments he had endured – the chemotherapy, radiotherapy, steroids, infections – and multiple medications and surgeries he had received over the five years had ultimately led to his death.

On 23rd December 2013, whilst Brett was in hospital

again, we were told there was nothing more they could do.

He 'came home' for the last time on Christmas Eve. He passed away on the 30th December 2013 at 5:22pm.

***

Brett's case was quite rare and equally severe, so I felt from virtually day one that the Grim Reaper resided on the roof of our home, strumming his fingers, waiting to see if he was going to take Brett or not.

Brett had had so many 'close calls', and had nearly passed away multiple times, that I thought he was quite super-human – Superman became his nickname. He repeatedly faced death during multiple ICU admissions, serious infections, anaphylactic shocks and every treatment side effect known to man (and a few side effects previously unknown to man) that I thought he must win.

In the end Brett's death was possibly kinder for him as he was free from the constant pain and suffering he had endured for over five long years, he had been so brave, but it was the beginning of a never-ending torture for us.

Chapter 2

Death Inconvenient?
Just a Tad

(This was the first of what was to be many children's deaths – lots of other children died before this one, but we were told they were alive and well by staff at the hospital. I'm not cross; I understand completely why they did it.)

***

3rd March 2011

I was woken up today, at 6:10am, by a text message from another cancer mum. We found out last night that John had relapsed again and was now terminal.

The shock has rocked my family to the core. John was in the bed next to Brett in hospital when he was first diagnosed. John had just started his treatment for the brain tumour. John is such a lovely boy, eleven years old, a Chelsea fan; he loves football, which is probably why he and Brett get on so well. John's mum and I had bonded immediately – well, let's be honest, you do as a cancer mum. There's no room for designer handbags and bragging about academic achievements in the child cancer ward. As long as you can force a smile and make a cup of tea, you are friends for life. We are all sisters and brothers in arms in the battle to save your very most precious child's life.

John has had such a hard time as well; he'd received an all-clear only for it to return for a third time, although it turns out now, it was actually a false all-clear.

I was so happy and relieved for John's mum when she told me last July about his scan results being all clear. She had told me about all of his terrible treatments and I had told her about Brett's; we had compared notes, as always. We had agreed to have lunch in the September when the children had gone back to school. I was supposed to call her. I was so happy that another 'tick' of success could go next to a cancer child we knew that I didn't call her in the September. Brett was continually ill and I felt it was unfair to bring her down with my day-to-day woes, as she had already been through too much. I decided to call her when Brett picked up. Little did I know that she had received the most startling news that the hospital had read his scan wrong and he would be gone by Christmas!

Brave John had held on through Christmas, but now he was very close to dying.

The real problem I have is the fact that I cannot stop crying. It is as if I have tapped into his mum's pain. I know she is at his bedside constantly, not wanting to move an inch away. She had said how unbearable the pain was that she felt; I agreed, but I had only glimpsed into that dark world on a couple of occasions, but Brett had always recovered. I, too, have sat next to Brett's bed in intensive care in the middle of the night willing him to live on multiple occasions, every inch of my being hoping and praying that it would be alright. I had felt my soul ache with pain at the very thought of him passing away. But I was OK; Brett had always pulled through and I was able to push those dark, terrifying moments to the back of my mind until now. All the darkest times of this horrendous long journey have come flooding back. I am overwhelmed with pain, fear and a heart-breaking sadness.

I have cried solidly for hours. Even now I feel guilty, because who am I to cry over someone else's child – what gives me the right?

"Be strong, pull yourself together, think of Brett and Poppy, straighten your knees… etc., etc." All that well-meaning positive crap keeps floating around my head. I'd like to see anyone try, try and constantly push their emotions down, suck it up, be positive and fake for week upon week, month upon month, year upon year. Well, today I've resigned from the 'it'll be OK' club, because sometimes it isn't. It's not OK that a beautiful, kind, funny, thoughtful boy is dying; it's not OK for a mother to lose her child – in any circumstances – but especially when she fought for so long to hold on to him, to just to have to sit and watch him slip away out of reach.

Cancer mums are just normal mums who have been thrown on a rollercoaster ride to hell which lasts years, and the only thing you pray for, as awful as every day is, is that you're still all together in the cart when the ride finally stops. We're not a special breed; we hurt so much and we're not stronger than anyone else. We're just better actors.

Our children are normal too. They are scared, they hurt and they get to a point almost daily where they've had enough of being ill. The small ones cry often; they cry when they see nurses because they know they're going to hurt them. They have tantrums and they scream; they howl and beg to be taken home away from the torture camp which is just a hospital clinic to you and me. Who could blame them? I think I could scream and wail for them. It's just not OK.

27th June 2011

I met John's mum today for the first time since his funeral. I was not expecting to hurt as much as I do. She scares me because she has endured one evil, dreadful step further than me. I found out from her about three other children we know who have died and I told her about all the ones at the hospital who've gone. Oh God, I've come home and cried loads, and I am still crying writing this. John's mum said she just wanted to hear his voice again and she would give anything to be in my shoes – my shoes?! Which, to me, are too painful to bear? I look at Brett and I get so afraid; he looks so frail and fragile, I feel so helpless, tiny and afraid. I know it's stupid and I need to strengthen up, but some days the best you can do is feel and acknowledge.

I really want vodka, cigarettes, pills – anything to mask the pain.

***

Brett came home from the hospital to die on Christmas Eve 2013; he was in slow multi-organ failure due to the treatment he had received for leukaemia for five and a half years. I had moved his bed downstairs to the front room. The house was decorated for Christmas, as I thought he would be coming home to enjoy Christmas and the rest of his life; I certainly didn't see his death coming.

The drugs for his end-of-life care had been brought in and placed in the hall ready for the nurses, who would pop in and out each day until he was gone. There were bags of stuff placed in the back room just under the Christmas tree. I looked inside one of the bags and saw that it was a large bag of brown-coloured towels. Later that day, I spoke to a palliative care nurse on the phone and asked what the towels were for; she replied they were in case he died by bleeding out – the colour of the towels might help mask it for our younger daughter.

I was in total shock and horror. *OH MY GOD! I am left alone with my beautiful child who is dying and it might be by him losing all his body's blood! Oh my God! I can't cope – this is like a horror show. I can't do it… I can't do this!* my mind screamed.

"OK," I replied calmly to her.

Although I hadn't believed that he would die for even one minute. *He's pulled a miracle out of the bag many times before during all those times in ICU and he'll do it again*, I'd thought.

But sadly, he was declining quickly, and I started to see and accept that this was going to be the end. My poor boy must have vomited and suffered diarrhoea every day of his life since he'd been diagnosed in September 2008. His tongue, the lining of the mouth and throat had been burnt off by chemo on a regular basis. He had suffered the most terrible side effects to the constant barrage of chemotherapy, then later radiotherapy and all the other drugs. He took hundreds of medications every day. He really had gone through the mill, and all for nothing, now it would seem. No one had battled like him or for as long as him; he was certainly our hero and a true warrior.

One morning we sat and talked as a family together about his death. We all needed to say as much as we could before the nurses arrived and started the permanent morphine pump. We said as much as we could through our tears. Brett told us what he wanted at his funeral and that he wanted his ashes to come home, to be with us, all together again. We each told him how much we loved him, but before we knew it, that was that.

The nurses arrived and his end-of-life treatment started. Kev and I had walked into the back room of our home; as the nurses saw to Brett, we broke down into each other arms but very quickly pulled back. We just acknowledged each other's pain with a single nod of the head. A nod that said we knew, but we also had to be strong.

I will never feel that I said or did enough for Brett, both during his life or around his illness and death.

At that time, I was trying to manage the situation rather than feel it. I was trying to console both my son and my daughter, who were desperately distraught with having to say goodbye to each other. I didn't have time to care about how I was feeling; I was too busy being their mother. We couldn't believe our beautiful boy, whom we had wanted and adored from a time way before he'd even arrived on Earth, was now going to be ripped away from us before our very eyes. Taken away after five and a half years of torture, pain and suffering, after we had all fought together so desperately hard to keep him here. We knew our life would now be over and would never be repaired once he had taken his last breath.

On the day he died it had been like the other days since he came home. Our family and friends had visited, and we had tried to make it as nice as possible; lots of jokes and laughter had flowed. But as this day progressed, the air became heavy.

To this day I can't explain what descended onto my house. Maybe the Grim Reaper was making his final preparations to leave for good, as since Brett's battle with cancer had started, I had felt that there had been a manic tug of war between us.

Brett himself hadn't changed much and was in and out of sleep, as he had been for the last few days. But my brother had sensed the feeling too. By 3:30 that afternoon my brother said that he thought they should all clear out and leave us alone, and I agreed; nothing more was said between us.

Brett, Poppy, Kev and I were all together in our living room for what was going to be the last time as a complete family. Kev and I sat on Brett's bed whilst Poppy sat just beside his bed. The room became strangely still; Brett lifted his head, turned and looked at something or someone that we couldn't see, and then he was gone, smiling at us as he went.

***

Death doesn't scare me now, as I know my son will be waiting for me. Although I am, like most people, frightened of just how I'm going to die. I am very scared of pain and loss of dignity. Of all the deaths I've been around – whether in a hospice, hospital or at home, and whether child or old person – I am yet to see a well-managed, calm, dignified death.

It shouldn't be this horrid in this modern era. It seems as though prolonging life at all costs is our only goal. Plans for death are still left in silence when really, we should be allowed to have some say on just how we will die. The choice should be ours, not the faceless state and hospital policy makers.

No one should have to travel to Dignitas in Switzerland because they want a dignified well-managed death. Dignitas's help is termed as an assisted suicide at present and that isn't available in the UK. A Dignitas death costs thousands of pounds and the person has to die much earlier than necessary because the patient has to be well enough to travel and be 'of sound mind' to legally sign the forms.

We should be able to write a purposeful and powerful living will that states things like:

- If I am at a place in my life journey where I no longer recognise my daughter and never will, then goodbye!
- If there's no chance of a full mental recovery, please end my life.
- If I'm in pain that will only get worse over time, please help me go quickly, when I've had enough.
- If I am an unresponsive cabbage, end my life.

Ye Gods! How patronising is it to live in a world that says, "OK, you have a degenerate disease; by the time you die, you will have spent a considerable amount of time being unable to communicate, feed yourself or wipe your own dribbling mouth or backside – but don't ask me to help you end your life, because I'm not allowed!"

No, we believe in life before death at any cost, even if that evaporates our basic human right to dignity. Did that degenerate disease scenario bring up pictures of a quality of life before death? ...I think not. Whether we like the concept or not, the truth is, a quick assisted death would often be a kinder death.

Yes, I am in favour of euthanasia – well, to be honest, I'm just totally against these cruel slow deaths which the majority of people don't even know exist until their cherished loved one is in the midst of it. You stand there open-mouthed, thinking there's got to be a better way than this, whilst the loved one suffers needlessly.

When Brett found out he was dying, he thought they (the hospital staff) would just come and give him an injection and he would fall asleep and die. When he found out he had to wait until his body had collapsed internally with all his organs ceasing to function properly, thereby making his body horribly toxic and God knows what else, he was devastated (he wasn't told about the chance of bleeding out, thankfully).

He said to us and the hospital staff, "I can't believe after everything I've gone through that even my death is allowed to torture me."

I didn't know what to say to him; I just mumbled, "I'm sorry," and I was. I felt I'd let him down so badly and I was such a failure that I couldn't even make him comfortable as he died. I carry the weight of that failure as a mum, but the 'system' has to share some of the blame too.

My friend has just had to watch her wonderful, lovely father die by a dementia death. It was downright evil. My friend's dad, had fallen at home and was taken to hospital by ambulance. The doctor seemed to think he had fallen due to muscle wastage. He didn't want to eat or drink in the hospital, although he had been eating quite happily at home. He just kept insisting he wanted to be allowed back home.

A few different doctors saw her father and they all agreed that he should be denied any IVs because it was dementia and there was no point prolonging his life anymore. They said he would die quickly, but, shockingly, it took three weeks of suffering.

He was on no medication whatsoever, no food, no drink, and when my friend questioned a nurse, she was told that he wasn't in any pain. Really? How did that nurse actually know? How could any professional really know for certain? The gentleman was moaning and restless, which showed there possibly was pain and, if not pain, there was definitely discomfort. There had been no visit from an end-of-life team because he stupidly dared to die in December.

Anyone linked to our health service knows that any holiday time is a dreadfully dangerous time to be in hospital. Oh, there are staff present in hospital, twenty-four hours a day, 365 days a year, but only the bare minimum needed for generally emergencies are present at holiday time. All the multi-disciplinary teams are not represented.

Another good friend of mine, who's spent two consecutive Christmases in hospital, didn't get seen by a member of the gastroenterology team which she so desperately needed to see and was the entire reason for her admittance into hospital, until way into the new year, on 6th January. Tragic when you think she started her hospital admission on 15th December. I don't class that as Christmas personally, but hey ho.

I have been in multiple hospitals over many holidays and it's always the same. The weekends were just as bad.

Brett would get sick on a Friday tea time and get a high temperature. The staff would take the blood tests from his central line that then needed to go to the labs (which grew the samples to see if any specific bugs appeared), but because it was the weekend the samples went in the fridge because the lab staff wouldn't be back until Monday.

So, my advice is: please try to remember Monday is obviously a far better day to get sick or try to die, as that's when the bulk of the staff are present.

Was it only because of the time of year that the wonderful, kind, gentleman had such a slow, vile dementia death? No, apparently not – it's the standard way they do it, even though it is an obvious case for assisted death. Do we as a society really feel it was humane to dry him out to kill him? They had to wait for his organs to shut down due to dehydration! I don't know much, but surely pain medication could have speeded the end up, and it certainly would have answered the 'is he in pain' question, wouldn't it?

When my son was at home dying, we found out that the doctors had to be careful not to overdose him. Overdose him! A palliative care patient – are you kidding me?!

Why? It's not murder, it's kindness. But it is against the law to assist someone to die and I guess that plays on these poor doctors' minds.

We need to grow up and manage death better as a whole society. State-controlled deaths need an urgent overview and need updating. These dark, dirty deaths need to stop and the palliative care failings need to be addressed. Death shouldn't be so nasty and degrading, as it all just adds to the overall fear of dying and death that people, quite rightly, have.

It's such a strange affair, because I wouldn't be allowed to let my dog suffer like we do humans. Could you imagine going to a vet and saying, "Yes, I know the dog is old and pretty useless, so I've decided I won't give it any food or water anymore, so it should die eventually."

The vet would call the authorities, as it's downright cruel. How disgusting is that realisation that people aren't treated as kindly as our own animals are!

I think people should be allowed to die peacefully and as quick as possible when the time comes. It would probably kinder for the family too.

Watching the carnage of a long, slow death is harrowing and it adds to the weight of guilt and shame when grieving.

'Could I have done more?' is the generic grieving person's question to themselves, specifically to the way the death was handled: "Should I have challenged the doctors to keep you more comfortable? Were you in pain? Did you suffer more than you should have? It was so dreadful – who knew the end of life would be like that? It's like being in a real-life horror movie," etc.

Death is so painful, even when it's expected and we know it's coming. It's time the whole ugly business was handled better and, at the very least, us mere humans should be allowed to have an individual choice and a say in the matter.

I might want a quicker ending whilst someone else might want to savour all the time they have left. Again, why is it a one-size-fits-all society?

My literal death wish is like so many other people's, which is to go to sleep here on Earth and wake up in heaven (or wherever). Nice and easy. If I should encounter some nasty disease that is going to have its wicked way with me until I die, then I want a managed death. I want to be able to say, "Enough now! Bring on the big guns, go get those drugs – goodbye, everyone."

I don't want my daughter having the vile images of my dark, painful death replaying endlessly in her head, especially when there's no need for it.

I wish people would take the time to think about death more. It is an integral part of our lives. We are all going to die; it is a certainty, yet it's rarely spoke about. Thinking about it and getting serious about death is actually quite invaluable and can enrich our lives. It brings the reality home to us all that we really don't have time to live a fake life. It's a sad message but also a powerful one.

There was a Buddha quote I really liked (until I found out it was fake – you've got to love the internet, but it's still a good quote): "The trouble is you think you have time."

Throw yourself into it today because it could all be over tomorrow. I wish I knew how life changes so quickly and to enjoy it more – I knew it but didn't *know* it as deeply as I do now. Death really is the ultimate game changer.

We should talk about death at an early age, and I'm sure it could be a subject for lessons and discussions, even in primary schools. If we can talk about sex in primary schools, then we can talk about death.

Let's grow up with regards to our attitudes and have some conversations about deaths from suicide too. I am surrounded by families of children and teenagers who battled like warriors for a chance to live in this world, yet died.

I feel suicide deaths are just the same. The cancer children fought a very physical, emotional and mental war; people who take their own life by suicide are fighting a terrifyingly invisible war, which no one seems to really understand.

I feel that referring to people who commit suicide as weak or selfish is absolute nonsense. No one in their right mind would take their own life, and yes, the clue is in the sentence, isn't it? 'In their right mind'.

I couldn't stand in front of a train and let it hit me, or jump off a building – are you kidding me? What mindset must you be in to do that? I've been to dark places in my head, but I've only ever contemplated suicide fleetingly.

True, I have wanted to escape the pain of Brett's death, but I equally couldn't inflict pain onto my husband, daughter and the rest of my family. I couldn't have tortured all those I'd left behind wondering what they could have, should have done to help me. For me, suicidal thoughts have gone out of my head as quickly as they've come into it.

So again, I ask what place mentally must these poor people be in to disregard the feelings of all those loved ones around them, knowing what pain their death will cause, and still do it anyway?

My theory is, I think their brain short wires like a sort of stroke or aneurism, but maybe it's deep inside the brain so it has not been discovered yet or perhaps something strangely chemical happens in the mind because suicide defies any logic and bypasses our primal urge for self-preservation.

No matter what the reason is, my heart hurts for them; they are desperately poorly people with an invisible illness. Their families suffer so much too. The added guilt and anger they must feel. "Why didn't they tell me? Why didn't they ask for help?"

For a parent not to be allowed to try and help their child (whatever their age) is just heart-breaking.

I feel so annoyed when families of suicide victims talk about their added shame – why shame? Suicide is the result of a disease that we don't yet understand. I hope we will one day, but we definitely don't understand it yet. There is nothing to be ashamed of. Which illness a person battled prior to death should make no difference to the people around you.

After Brett's cancer diagnosis, we had a lot of conversations about death as a family. Poppy and Brett had already lost Grandad Bert years before, but as a 'grandad', it didn't really spark too many deep conversations other than it was the 'circle of life' and he had been ill for a long time (he had suffered many strokes). The general theme was people get old and die. My children were encouraged to talk about Grandad whenever they wanted to and cry if they missed him. It was a neat and tidy circle of life and death, and it was better than watching him continue to suffer.

When Brett started losing his young cancer friends, that affected him (and us) greatly. He grieved for more friends in his short life than most of the adults I know. Every time there were no words to comfort him because it was just all too tragic.

He and his fellow cancer friends would put most adults to shame with their level of grace and decorum at the different and very many funerals they attended when honouring their fellow fallen warriors.

It's simply not the same when the circle of life fucks up and the deceased was too young to die. Young deaths definitely seem to hurt more because they are intrinsically wrong: children shouldn't die; it's not the right way.

A palliative care nurse who organised Brett's release home from the hospital warned us about all of the people who would suddenly show up out of nowhere once he had passed away. It was part of her remit to guard us against the huge outpouring that would happen once the news of his death spread.

She didn't know if it was because the deaths she dealt with were children, or children with cancer, but it was almost as if the whole community around you wanted to mourn with you, albeit for an incredibly small amount of time.

She likened it to a sad form of rubbernecking. It's similar to when the people on the opposite side of the road slow down to stare at a road traffic accident; we were that car crash.

People did express their condolences after Brett died. I don't remember it being too excessive, but then again, I didn't really notice. My lovely boy had just died; I couldn't have cared less what the world around me was doing.

The five years of horror, pain and suffering Brett had endured made me feel as though his death was his escape. *Fly away baby, and be free – they can't hurt you anymore*, I'd thought after his death, and the thought still brings me a tiny bit of comfort now.

Those first days were strange. I felt cold, dark, numb, breathless, detached, as though I was in a void, in some parallel existence.

Even then for me, I felt the initial months following Brett's death, with its mixture of pain and debilitating numbness, were far better than the following years of pain and searing anger.

Now, I open my eyes in the morning and the first thing that hits me is: he's gone. Sometimes, after an obviously good dream, I can imagine he's still here. I can imagine he's safely tucked up in his bed and will soon be demanding breakfast of red sauce on toast (yuk, I know, don't ask). Then, the truth seeps in like a cold damp fog. *He's dead, Sarah*, a voice says in my head, and the very familiar feeling of doom takes hold again – yep, ready for another day.

Death caused so many evil emotions, but for me I was so overwhelmingly exhausted. The battle had been too long and hard, and the total disbelief that he'd actually gone took a long time to dissipate.

I honestly thought my son was going to make it. After all, we were good people. He was a lovely, kind, generous person. He had to make it – what would I ever do without him? I was brought up on a diet of Hollywood-style films with happy endings. In those stories the good guy always wins and the bad guys don't. In my life, exactly the opposite happened.

It's not fair; it's not right; it shouldn't be happening this way. Yes, of course I knew bad things happened to good people, but not to *us*! Not my family. We were good people – what went wrong? How come my lovely, kind son was dead and shit-bag horrible people still walk this Earth?

My son's death is nothing but a waste.

He would have been a huge asset to this world; he was wonderfully clever, nice, kind and generous – one of life's good kids.

But the weird thing was, they all were. We were surrounded on those cancer wards by nice, loving, kind, generous, respectful families and their children, who were fighting cancer. They were breath-taking and outstanding. I never met a child I didn't like on those wards. I attended a lot of their funerals too and all I can say is, what an unbelievable, total and utter waste. They all would have changed the world in a very good way.

Throughout those treatment years I believed each battle Brett won meant he was one day closer to a cure and his freedom from illness when the real truth was, with each day that passed, Brett was one day closer to death and freedom from illness.

You're simply never ready for someone to die, even if they've been ill for years and it could possibly be a relief for the person themselves; you just can't prepare for it.

Any death is multi-faceted, as that person is many different people. I lost a son; Poppy lost her brother, sparing partner and best friend; Brett's friends lost a peer, and for some of them it was also a major life-changing event.

In the cancer community Brett's death caused a lot of shock and worry, as Brett had been 'Superman' and survived so much that his passing greatly upset those who were still undergoing treatment. I was very worried about the young people around Brett after he passed. I couldn't imagine what I would be like if I had seen everything that they had witnessed at their young ages.

Brett's body was taken to the funeral home on the same evening of his passing. After he had gone the three of us sat on the sofa in our living room just staring at Brett's empty bed. Poppy slept with us in our bed that night. We were all in shock, disbelief and agony that he had gone. I lay there that night and made a silent promise that it was Poppy's turn now. I had focused relentlessly on Brett during his long and arduous battle and knew I needed to focus on Poppy in the same way now. My poor girl. No one her age should have witnessed the horrors she had seen; she shouldn't have attended so many cancer children funerals who had become her friends too, and now she was to attend her only brother's funeral.

The fall-out after a young person's death is very large and widespread, albeit with most people not knowing how to process it all. After Brett died, apart from close friends and family, stony silence was normally what we were greeted with when we went out into the world. It was a serious case of bereavement leprosy. People had the facial expression I can only describe as a rabbit caught in a car headlight.

People looked terrified. It wasn't a look of 'blessed are the grieving' – no, it was more like, "Oh, shit, they're coming this way, I need to make a sharp exit," and as they were hastily making their retreat from us, they would throw a comment over their shoulder like, "Call me if… erm, you need anything," which, roughly translated, meant: "Please don't call, or maybe in a year or two."

If people did stop and talk to us, they would still try and quote the 'feel better'-type clichés that have been banded around for years, and I guess they might possibly soothe a little when someone older dies, but they definitely don't work in the case of a young person dying.

"He had a good innings." I would think or say, depending on what mood I was in, *You didn't come to the cancer ward, did you? He really didn't have a good innings at all.*

"Time heals." *Yes, it will take the exact amount of time to heal me as it takes for me to have died and spent my first day in heaven.*

"There are no words." *True, except swear words.*

"What can I say?" *Apparently nothing worth listening to, judging by that comment.*

"He was too good for this Earth." *Seriously?! What rubbish.*

"Call me when you're feeling better." *I've lost my son; I'm not suffering with tonsillitis.*

"I know how you feel." *No, you don't! You still have your children! OMG, please don't start talking about when you lost the cat – just stop talking!*

"God only takes the best; he needed his special angel back." *Oh, step back, sweetie, I'm going to punch you in your smug face, and FYI, your God's a bastard.*

In this advanced world we live in, we arrogantly believe we can solve everything, but the truth is we can't, especially when it comes to death and grieving. People don't understand that for a newly bereaved person they often only need support – that's all, just support.

People don't know how to just support each other properly. Well, the secret is, it's all about them, not you. To support someone else, you must try and put them first and foremost, and that's a pretty tough call in this 'me, me, me' world. People today seem to view situations whilst asking themselves, *What's in it for me? Where's the payoff?* It takes a special person to stay with a friend when the bottom of their world's fallen out.

Unless, of course, they are the rubberneckers, those people who thrive in times of misery and despair. "Let me help," they cry. "Give me all the gory details," they say as their eyes widen in anticipation. But the rubberneckers are also only involved for their own needs, not to provide you with any true help.

The bereaved need people to be calm and just listen for a change – be quiet. Not spewing 'what you wanna do is'-type advice and 'when I lost Mum I did this, this and this'. Remember it's their bereavement, not yours. Shut up unless you're asked your opinion or a direct question.

Don't presume you know anything that could help the person and if you really want to help, simply just let them be, do and say whatever they want to.

Let them drink if they want to, or not; eat if they want to, or not; sleep if they want to, or not. Basically, just shut the fuck up and just be there for them.

"There are no words," is a nice statement to make to a grieving person because it is true but as long as it's used as part of a longer conversation that involves listening to the bereaved person, as opposed to just a throw away comment as I mentioned before.

"I'm sorry for your loss," which means I'm sorry you're hurting – universally nice and kind.

"I'm here for you and whatever you need," is lovely, but again, only say it if you mean it and can be there for them.

Grief isn't deadly; it doesn't kill us, but it is the strangest, most powerful thing we will ever experience, and just because I did certain things doesn't mean anyone else will. Maybe we need to learn to trust ourselves individually a bit more and stop looking constantly outside for soothing and for someone who may have all the answers. No one has all the answers.

Most people see their friend's true colours when they have their first bereavement. But Brett's long-term illness had enabled me to already see people for what they mostly were, which was wimps who ran when the going got tough.

Straight after an initial life-altering diagnosis there are people everywhere. You make endless cups of tea for visitors, and answering all the calls and texts becomes quite exhausting, but then, within a few weeks and months, people just slope off. They stop calling in, they stop calling on the phone, then you get the occasional text. "What's happening now, update me when you're free," which eventually becomes a 'no response required or wanted'-type text: "Thinking of you," or, "You're in my thoughts."

By the time Brett died, I had given up on most of my friends and family. It's a sad truth that people are very busy, and illness and death are, frankly, a buzzkill, the ultimate downer. The resentment I felt was deep and powerful. My large army of good friends had turned into a sea of deserters, and that sometimes did make me feel quite bitter.

Ironically, people acted as if death was something only I was ever going to experience. Noooo, please! Everyone will feel the wrath of the Grim Reaper at some point in their lives. It'll happen over and over again if you live long enough. No one is immune to the touch of death.

I often feel very alone grieving in this fast-paced world, where people are friends on Facebook yet ignore you in the street. I know my experience is no different to most of the people I talk to. Strangers who have gone through what you're experiencing are often a far better resource for you than your closest friends. Nothing beats a true and honest interaction with someone who really understands. "I know, I've been there, I'm still there, I understand."

With general society, though, it's just a case of 'laugh and the world laughs with you, cry and you cry alone'.

But please remember you are not alone, there are millions of sad and grieving people on this planet today. We need to find a way and connect and talk about our loved ones with each other; you can contact me on the Facebook page 'Because of Brett the Book'.

As an endnote, though – please don't be put off seeking support if you need it. There is support out there if you are feeling very lonely or you are struggling badly; you just have to go and find it. Start with your GP or doctor, or contact your local bereavement support group or the Samaritans.

Chapter 3

Putting the Fun in Funerals

During those initial days after someone passes away, it always amazes me just how the mind is able to switch from abject horror and wildly despairing thoughts to clinically and coldly sorting out the physical side of death. Everyone manages to get all the stuff done that needs doing for the deceased loved one, and there's a lot to do. Just at a time when you could do with sitting and resting, you have to decide on or find out what to do with the deceased's remains, arrange a funeral, which more often than not is excellently thought out, with interesting stories and anecdotes about the deceased.

Then, there's the financial side of it all, and ultimately what to do with the deceased's possessions. It's the very worst time of your life, yet you still get it all done. There is a strength that pushes you on, but I don't know where it comes from.

I recently attended the funeral of my friends' father He had passed away at ninety-four years old and had suffered with dementia. Anyone who knows about dementia knows that the end was simultaneously very sad and a quiet relief. It's a terrible illness that affects the whole family, not just the sufferer. He had died in hospital, and due to it being winter, there was a backlog of people who had died; subsequently the funeral had taken a whole calendar month before it could take place. This is a terrible situation for the family. Most people who've lost a family member prefer a quicker funeral than a whole month.

The funeral was a lovely, respectful and dignified event, which was a perfect representation of the gentleman that he was. Trouble was, I had 'lost it' completely. I had been 'good' during the funeral service, and by good, I mean not crying. He was a lovely man, but he was ninety-four years old, and compared to all the children funerals I've been to, and to not sound too cold or callous, it wasn't the saddest affair. Obviously, it was terribly sad for the close family, but it was one of those occasions where you could say one of those awful clichés: "He had a good life," and, "A good innings," as it were.

The funeral had taken place in Brett's chapel (where Brett had had his funeral). It's not like it is his chapel because, truth be told, they are more like the Grim Reaper's conveyor belts. I had known prior to the day that it was his chapel, so it's not like it was a sudden shock. The funeral was over and the family wanted to be left alone with the coffin for a few minutes, so the congregation was asked to go outside. As I walked outside through the chapel door I completely broke down into hysterics. The minister, who was holding the door open for us to leave, looked aghast. He must have thought that my emotions were completely over the top for a general mourner to have.

The truth was, as I exited the building, I seemed to have a complete flashback to Brett's funeral. At that time, I had been determined not to cry at Brett's funeral as there were so many children attending (both healthy and cancer kids still undergoing treatment), and I knew that once I start crying, I'm very emotional and I can't seem to stop. I really wish I could cry like some ladies do, with a little tear that slowly escapes from the corner of their eye that they then gently wipe away.

Instead, I cry really ugly, sobbing and gasping for breath, unable to speak, usually accompanied by a bright red face, and my already small eyes all but disappear. It's quite the sight to see, but not in a good way; it's more like watching irate people argue – it's quite repulsive and definitely not polite to stare, but you just can't bring yourself to look away.

In the case of my friend's funeral, the tears I suppressed over Brett's funeral seemed to release all at once, albeit many years later. There I was, stood outside a chapel, being a hysterical mess at a funeral that I shouldn't have been so upset at. People around me stared with wide eyes and puzzled looks on their faces. I eventually staggered over to the chapel car park, where I was able to slowly pull myself together. It took quite a while to gather what was left of my decorum and re-join the mourners, but I knew I would be joining them with a bright red face, as that takes an absolute age to calm down. *Nice one, Sarah*, I thought to myself. *How classy.* I guess you've got to laugh. Brett would be laughing, as would the man whose funeral it was.

The next funeral I attended was my auntie's. She was a lovely lady. Her funeral was so very nice (if you can say that about a funeral? But I think you know what I mean). After the funeral there was the usual wake, which again was nice because it meant having a catch-up with family. I hadn't seen my lovely, rather large, extended family for a while. It was probably Brett's funeral when I had seen them last. It does appear that our family seems to meet at weddings, christenings and funerals, with the latter being the worse, obviously.

Throughout our grieving Brett, we have continued to make jokes, just as we had through his illness (Brett was the absolute worse culprit for finding the funny side in things that just weren't appropriately funny) and it would seem that this day was going to be no exception. That's how we as a little family cope, always with humour, but most people can't laugh at gallows humour because they find it too uncomfortable. Each to their own, and I was probably the same before Brett's illness.

Anyhoo, we were at the wake and all sitting chatting in small groups when Poppy, who was on the other side of the room, started trying to indicate something to me by mouthing words as she didn't want to shout over the room. It turned into a sort of game of charades. I eventually understood what she was saying (which was about taking my father home in the car), but I teased her and pretended I couldn't get fully what she was saying, which in turn made her a little mad and irritated. It was amusing to begin with, but then she started getting really animated, so I mouthed that it was OK, I understood what she was trying to say. Then I said to the group around me, who had by now stopped talking to each other and were watching us, "You see! What can you do? The good one died!" I chuckled whilst it felt like the whole room simultaneously gasped in horror.

My cousin whispered hurriedly, "You can't say that."

I replied, "Why not? It's just a joke, and of course I don't mean it for one minute." I could tell I had shocked the people around me, but I wasn't actually sure if it was because I had jokingly put Poppy down or referred to Brett being dead. I often feel as though there's an unwritten rule that referencing the dead is a really bad show and bad manners. Anyway, I guess I had done it again; I seem to have recurring 'foot in mouth' syndrome.

It's also strange, whilst talking about serious illness, a death or a funeral, how many times you inadvertently can include inappropriate words in a sentence: you're dead against something, dead on time, dying to see that, dying to get in there, made a grave mistake, buried in things to do, got burned, a burning question, not a morning (mourning) person, guess my humour's too grave, a dead giveaway, dead-end job, over my dead body, that is dead hard, that will be the death of me.

These are but a few examples, and there are many more because I am the queen of saying stupid things at the worst of times. My jokes, quite rightly, tend to go down like a lead balloon.

During all the funerals I've attended since Brett's funeral, I have made some observations that makes me never want to attend any funeral ever again (which is, again, a stupid thing to say because it's not that I look forward to them anyway. "Oh, goody, the neighbours died, bring on the funeral whoop, whoop."). I am now terrified of attending funerals in case I 'release the beast' that resides inside me. Funerals trigger a darkness in me that I spend most normal days busily trying to sink down. The depth of my grief is endless whilst mostly private and personal, whereas funerals are, in contrast, very public affairs.

The first funeral you ever attend is a very frightening event. Depending on your age you may have seen funerals depicted in shows and films and heard about them, but attending your first one is far more difficult than you usually expect. There's the traditions within every culture and religion that need to be adhered to and respected; you need to find your place in the pecking order, as it were; and then there comes controlling yourself because no one can verbally warn you enough about the physical effect of the collective emotions from all the other mourners and how that affects your emotions, regardless of how close or not you were to the deceased. I think you can spot a first-timer a mile off despite their age. They have very wide (normally very red) eyes and look quite terrified as if they were about to go to their own death. Mourners around them instinctively guide these first-timers by gently herding them along and passing them hymn books, tissues, etc.

I believe that all the very sad and powerful emotions from every funeral we've ever attended are collected in a sort of mental barrel which we are then able to put the lid back on after the event is over at varying speeds.

Sometimes the lid is put back on the emotional barrel very quickly, even as early as by the time the funeral is over. Times such as the deceased just being a neighbour or distant relative, someone who you've not got a close bond with and who, if you're honest, you're probably not really going to miss very much and them dying won't have affected your life. You just wanted to pay your respects. Although the funeral may have upset you and brought back some sad emotions, it really is not going to affect you for more than that day or so.

When a person dies who is close to you and you are going to miss them terribly in your life, then those are the times when the lid comes off the barrel and it takes a lot longer for the lid to be put back on. It can take months or sometimes years before the grieving person feels a bit more back to who they were before the lid came off and 'grief' became their normal way of life. Then sometimes there's people like me who knows the lid will never go back on the barrel completely; with its sad and raw emotion, it is a part of me now. It's something I will live with until my death. I just wish I could control myself in front of others, as I really hate any attention, but there's just no getting over the death of my little (5'11") boy.

Brett knew he was dying and wanted to plan some of his own funeral. He was a huge fan of *The Big Bang Theory* and loved the character Sheldon Cooper. In the show Sheldon has a line about 'putting the fun in funerals'. Brett had joked about that for years.

When he was dying Brett said he wanted us to put the fun in his funeral. I must admit it actually put the fear of God into me. I wanted to rip out my heart and stamp on it because it hurt so much and here was my brave son saying his farewell should be a party. I didn't know how I was going to pull that off, but I would do anything for him. He said the people attending should wear either his beloved football team's colours, which is sky blue, or something Superman, which was his nickname. No one wearing the colour black (which is the English traditional colour of mourning) as that was too dreary. He had said it all with a smile and I saw he found it highly amusing.

I had struggled to find something to wear that was a good enough tribute to him. Poppy had a lovely Superman T-shirt and Kev had the football shirt from their beloved team, so they were sorted, but I couldn't find anything I thought would make him proud, so in the end I stopped trying to make him proud; instead I decided to honour the 'fun in funeral' ethos Brett loved so much. Brett's order of service had a picture of him in hospital wearing a Superman onesie, so that was what

I wore to his funeral. I wore that very same Superman onesie, although it looked way better on him, but I hope it made him laugh as that was the intent.

People gave me very strange looks, but to be fair, a grieving mother can get away with anything – the gloves are off from society; there are no rules anymore. This kind of makes you feel worse, as everyone feels safer with boundaries, but society's expectations of you disintegrate when your child dies.

I wore the fluffy onesie and red wellies to my son's funeral. My brother had bought me the wellies; I didn't even think of my feet, as the onesie had the feet included as part of it. Shows he was cleverer than me, as it was early January in England, which is definitely not a conducive time of year to just have only cloth on your feet.

Weirdly enough, we actually did laugh a lot whilst organising Brett's funeral. Funny stories and memories we shared as a family kept popping into our minds. You expect to cry constantly when someone dies. You don't expect to laugh; it seems wrong and a bit disrespectful to admit it, but I guess it reflected our (mostly) happy life together. We laughed a lot together in life, so why not laugh in death?

I'd become obsessed, over the weeks prior to it, about giving Brett the best funeral ever. It would be the last time I could show him and the world just how special he was. I worked tirelessly on videos, pictures, orders of service, and even the minister's service was written by me. Every last detail mattered.

The minister was a lovely lady whom we had met in hospital. Brett didn't believe in God when he died; he had suffered too much by then, and I really don't blame him. He had told the minister this when she had come to visit him in his hospital room one day, but she had just gently laughed and said that it didn't stop her from visiting him, and besides, she believed in God enough for the both of them. They became good friends and Brett liked her a lot, so we were over the moon when she said she would conduct his funeral. I had written up a series of stories and anecdotes about Brett so that she had a variety she could choose from, and we loved the fact that she knew him personally, which is not always the case at funerals.

I know Brett didn't believe in God when he died, and I had definitely lost my faith over the evil previous years, and even though I was hugely mad at God if he did exist at all, I still wanted him represented at the funeral. I felt a huge urge to hedge our bets, just in case there was a God and he punished Brett even more in death than he had already in life, because he had had a non-Christian funeral (I don't know, even as I'm writing this I know it all sounds so stupid, but it was a classic case of do what feels right, so I did).

I asked if the cross could stay in the chapel during the service and that we said prayers for Brett; I also had the proper Christian committal, although we didn't have the coffin moved immediately after. Our chapel has the automated metal rollers, and sometimes at different funerals I've seen the coffin rolled along and moved to behind the curtains after the committal – it's a little bit too James Bond-movie-dramatic for me. I didn't want the children attending to be distressed any more than they already were.

We had all attended Jay's funeral a couple of weeks before Brett died and the crosses were taken out of the chapel for his service. The parents wanted no representation of a god that had tortured then taken their child. Jay was a lovely boy who had been a close friend of Brett's on the ward during the last year of Brett's treatment and life. To think they both died within weeks of each other is shocking.

We attended the funerals of so many cancer children that we had to start not attending some. The pain of a child's funeral is immense and we had already attended about ten before we found that we just couldn't do it anymore. The emotional toll was starting to really get to us. Some weren't called funerals, just 'their special days', but they're all celebrations of their lives that were cut down by child cancer and, basically, just too sad. These were the brave warriors that had fought shoulder to shoulder with each other and they were quietly passing away one by one. We were also very protective of each family at the funerals of these children. We would look around at the huge crowds of people attending and think, *Where have you all come from? We never saw any of you on the hospital ward actually visiting the child.*

It's all a bit too much, and you fear sometimes that your pain can become others' sick entertainment.

So many children died, it became a rarity when one lived. The child cancer world is a dark place that I walked away from after Brett's death and I have never looked back. Some parents start charities in honour of their children to help other children with cancer – good for them, but we just couldn't stay there anymore. Five and a half years was long enough for us.

Brett's funeral for me was more like a very public performance than a funeral. I was show-casing my beautiful, heroic boy and all he'd achieved in his way-too-short life, and I had only a small amount of time to do it in. I wasn't going to use his funeral for personal grieving, as I had the rest of my life to do that. We paid the chapel for extra slots because we didn't want to be rushed out and away. You do spend a lot of money on a child's funeral, as it's the last time you're going to get to spend money on them. There is no grand, special birthdays to buy for and celebrate, no weddings, no house deposits and no grandchildren. No 'thing' ever again.

A lot of the child funerals we had attended had been huge events with live bands playing music, loads of food and things like balloon releases to follow. I tried to fuse my more spiritual beliefs and aspects with old traditions. I wanted spirituality and Christianity to sort of merge, so we had arranged a white dove release for after Brett's committal. Four doves were to be released to symbolise his spirit going up to heaven; it was to be one each for the father, the son, the Holy Spirit and Brett's soul. It was actually a huge disaster, but it turned out to be a very funny one.

It's often said that the spirit of our departed loved one attends their own funeral, so I planned Brett's funeral with that in mind. *Hope he likes this and that*, I kept thinking to myself.

When their grandparents died, he and Poppy loved it when we would be talking about them and the house lights would flicker. If it was only a coincidence then it was a really good one because it would only happen when we were talking about them. Brett and Poppy used to look around and say, "Wow they're really here." It was fun but also a sign from those in heaven, I thoroughly do believe.

During Brett's funeral there were a couple of videos to play; the lights were put out for the first video then they were to be put back on after it finished. When they were put back on, the lights flickered. Kev, Poppy and I quickly looked at each other and smiled because we thought that was a sign from Brett, then the lights on a chandelier just went out. We could see someone in the background trying to put the lights on again but obviously decided to leave it, as it was only one chandelier out and there were others, plus there was a funeral going on. After the final video all the lights fused; we don't think many people even noticed as it wasn't a dark day outside, but we did. We all thought it was a clear sign from Brett.

After the service we walked outside to the gardens for the dove release; the gentleman who owned the doves came rushing over, apologising profusely, saying that for the first time in his twenty years in business the doves had escaped. He was going back to get more doves and we should just hang on for a little while. We all thought it was very funny and wondered if they had maybe had help escaping. It would be typical of Brett and his now-heavenly group of mischievous friends, acting just as they had been on the cancer wards together.

Whilst on the hospital wards these kids weren't sweet little angels as they are so often depicted; they were normal teenagers (well, they tried to be). They had teenage strops, loved their mobile phones, loved playing video games, loved playing pool and one of the games they liked playing a lot was with nerf guns (these are the guns that shoot soft foam bullets), and as loving parents we would join in, normally by being target practice for them. I have to admit, some of our large battles across the ward, which included all the families, were very funny. You had to just make the best of it in there. All the kids had their own nerf guns and occasionally, when they had eaten their tea and had been given their millions of medications, blood transfusions and chemo, etc., the friendly war games would begin in earnest.

Looking up into the tree that day after Brett's funeral and seeing those white escaped doves all in a row made us all think of those friends. When the gentleman returned with another four doves to do the release properly, all the doves went off together, including the original ones who had been waiting in the trees. They all circled together above us for quite a while then flew off into the distance; it was beautifully poignant.

Very bad admission, but I normally quite enjoy a good wake (the reception after a funeral); they're usually a welcome release, the place to relax and share the funny stories and good times spent with the deceased. But

Brett's was awful. I couldn't stand watching everyone laughing and smiling and enjoying themselves whilst my boy was left behind in the cold chapel. I wanted to know where he was, as I knew he wasn't really in that body, but where was he? Was he OK? I hoped he thought we'd done him proud at his funeral.

I couldn't wait to go home. I wanted to go home and close the door and never open it again. Which is pretty much what I did.

The day after the funeral would have been Brett's nineteenth birthday. He was diagnosed with leukaemia at thirteen years old and had lived in and out of hospital ever since. He spent his wonderful eighteenth birthday in total isolation after he'd had his first bone marrow transplant. The local paper wrote a story on him because it was so sad. We didn't really care, as we were used to 'sad'. Brett had spent most Christmases, holidays and birthdays in hospital and ill since he'd started treatment. We got used to it in a way; as long as we could all be together, we didn't really care, plus we always thought he would beat the cancer and win! We told him that he had plenty of time to celebrate his eighteenth and further birthdays once the transplant had worked – what little we knew.

We had put one copy of the cards we were giving Brett for his birthday in his coffin the night before his funeral when we 'supposedly' said our final farewells. I wasn't sold on the idea of goodbye. I will never say goodbye to my son.

We put the other copy of his birthday cards up in the living room and spent the rest of his birthday feeling hollow, cold and sad. We were blissfully unaware that the real grieving was just beginning.

For most people the funeral is the alleged signal that it's time to move on and start healing; for us there was no chance of that. There would be no healing nor moving on. Brett's funeral was a celebration of him and his life, and we intend to continue celebrating until we die.

He will forever be never forgotten.

Chapter 4

Grief, You've Got a Friend in Me

12th March 2015

What has to happen for me to feel good?

Brett has to be here, my mind instantly answered. Brett has to have lived, but instead he's dead and everything's ruined; my whole life is ruined. I don't want to win the lottery; I just want my son to be alive. God, please bring my son back.

I am so tired. I am angry and feel worthless and useless and a failure. Everything feels dirty and shabby; I have no motivation and think, *What's the fucking point?* to anything. I hate feeling this sad; I want to run away, but from what exactly?

Me, I think, and the sadness. I want to be one of those people who smile at memories of their loved ones, not fall into a gaping hole of pain.

I look at the people of the world and just see a hollow sham. Money, power, fame and wealth – so what? Nothing has importance; it's the people you love who matter.

Things! What's the deal with all the things? People are obsessed with buying crap, filling their homes with stuff, then posting a picture of it on social media. Who cares? Fucking stupid life.

Sorry, Brett, your mum was a complete failure, I couldn't save you, I'm so sorry, I love you baby xxxx

***

If you are reading this, I should imagine it's because you have lost someone you love and adore and are grieving the loss. If that's the case, then please accept my sincerest condolences; I am very sorry for your loss. I am very sorry for everyone's losses, whether expected or sudden, whether young or old, whether animal or human.

Death hurts so badly. Grief is terrible and frightening, but it needn't be. We need to learn to talk about death and accept it as the only thing we are all guaranteed to experience. We are all going to die one day, but our own death is often not as frightening as losing someone we love. We are all going to lose people we love and adore, and we will grieve those losses, yet we will all experience grief in very different and unique ways because we are all individuals.

It's a sad fact then that death is still mostly a taboo subject in modern society.

How is it that generations after generations of thinkers have industrialised the world, have been able to make huge advances in medicine, solved epic problems with maths and physics, put people in rockets and sent them into space, yet still cannot hold a decent conversation about death? It's as though death is not a given path for us all but instead our biggest human failure.

Since I was a child, I've heard multiple news reports about how scientists believe that one day a human will be able to live forever. As if eternal life is our only and most important goal. Well, I guess if everyone lives forever then we've solved the problem of death.

I personally don't want to live forever, as my son is dead. He's already gone home and I will follow him when it's my time. I believe he exists somewhere, in spirit and energy form, somewhere in this huge universe or maybe even in another dimension. Who knows? Where we go after we die remains one of life's biggest questions.

I think I get little messages and signs from Brett: a white feather will flutter down in front of me, a butterfly will pause near me, a penny will appear in the weirdest of places and sometimes I think I can feel Brett's presence around me and in our home.

But in reality, so what! Who cares? I can't hug him, I can't text him and ask him about his day, I can't laugh with him, and I can't kiss his beautiful soft cheek whilst he playfully resists after laughingly shouting, "Oh, Mum, get off," and then exaggeratedly wipes the kiss away. Signs are not enough, but they are going to have to be because that's the best I'm ever going to get from now on.

I live with grief; I live with the missing, the empty, very painful ache inside of me. I will never feel complete again; I will never be fulfilled again, as one of my children isn't here anymore. My ducks will never be in a row again, as I've lost one of my precious ducklings. As a mother, I think it's the ultimate failure. I most certainly do not want to live forever; sometimes my only solace is the fact that one day we will all be with him again.

I died the day my son died; that version of me is gone. I lost who I was around him and how he made me feel when we were together. I've lost being able to share my time with him and do the fun, practical, real-life things together. I hate the fact that he now only exists in a time gone past, in a previous life. He is my history when I want him in my present and future. I get to talk about him now only as a fading shadow, and it sucks big time.

I've lost that human bond with him, that here-and-now togetherness, and it's so sad; I miss him so much, and that missing is a very real and physical pain.

We generally live in a society now where we don't have to ever feel pain that we can't escape from. In an abusive marriage? Then leave. Have a headache? Take painkillers. Hate your job, home, school, parents, life? Then change it, leave it. We are quite rightly taught to move away from anything that causes us pain. We are the free generation that does not have to do anything we don't want to. "It's all about me and how I feel, and I have the human basic right to be safe and happy."

All of which is brilliant – why should we have to suffer and feel pain in our lives unnecessarily? But when a person we love dies, we are thrown into chaos, a scary, painful darkness that we are not equipped to cope with, coupled with an unhelpful society that is death-phobic.

There is no escape from grief; pop the pill, run away, hit the bottle if you want to, but just know that pain will always be there, waiting.

When you think about it, our brains are the most amazing machines, simultaneously instructing blood to be pumped around the body, our immune system to be vigilant for signs of infection, our cells to be oxygenated and renewed whilst all the time thinking, receiving information, analysing it, then deciding what to do with it. Excellent stuff, until you arrive at a dark, disturbing subject like death. Faced with death, the mind goes haywire. When dealing with the death of a loved one, the mind spirals out of control and, coupled with the presence of the combined effects of the emotional and physical responses too, in short, you've got holy hell.

Initially when someone dies, the emotions can be just disbelief and general resistance to the horror: "This can't be happening, this isn't true, no way." People often talk about the need to see the body of someone who's passed 'for closure' and to rule out that nagging voice in their mind still whispering, "It's not true, they've made a mistake, mistakes happen."

When you've accepted it's them and they've actually died, the initial feeling was, for me, like falling into a black hole. I wanted to scream, but in reality, I could barely even speak, and the feelings I had were very like panic rising, total fear, with a cold feeling of impending doom. I know that sounds melodramatic, but that was how I felt for days after Brett died.

I would honestly say from those initial moments onwards you could produce a huge list of every negative emotion known to man and I probably experienced all of them at some point. Some stay, some go quickly and some just flicker through, but none were either predictable or comfortable.

People are quite desperate for a guide or timeframe to help them understand what's happening, but grief doesn't work to a neat and tidy framework; grief is messy and extremely individual. There is no straight line, no steadfast course you will follow. Everything and anything that is happening, as strange and uncomfortable as it may seem, is OK and normal. Well, I think 'nothing feels or is normal' describes the grief process better. Grief takes a solid floor and makes it shaky as if it's moving underneath your feet. *This isn't* me, is a recurring thought, but sadly it is you now. Death changes us, even if only for a short while.

Have you planned your own funeral? I bet the answer is no. Do your loved ones even know what to do with your remains or how you would like to be remembered? Where you want to be laid to rest, or scattered, maybe? Cremation or burial are the bare minimum your loved ones should know. For most of society, death is a subject that they are extremely squeamish about. The only time death is discussed normally is to tell a person to not wallow in grief and get over it.

The general societal expectation is one of, "You'd better move on fast, sweet pea."

Because you will see very quickly that even if you don't, your friends and family certainly will.

Sure, they're all hearts and kisses initially after someone dies, but the day after the funeral, they'll be more like Road Runner – beep, beep.

They'll all leave so fast they'll be skid marks on the road outside your home.

I don't feel it should be this way. Death is a part of life and there are billions of people out in the world silently suffering because they should be 'over it' by now and unsurprisingly they're not.

The truth is, nothing works to soothe or comfort the grieving person, which generally lets society off the hook. "If nothing's going to work, then I guess don't need to try," people falsely assume.

It's a strange time in our lives and for a while with grief there's nothing to be said or done – it just is. People could just come by and 'be' there for us and with us, though.

I've seen some people grieve more over their pet than their parents. I don't judge – perhaps their pets were more loving. We grieve about what we think, and feel we've lost, whether it's a real, loving parent or the loss of the chance of a good relationship with a parent.

We grieve for all our tomorrows. We grieve for things that were probably never going to happen anyway. But whilst the person was alive, there was always a chance. We grieve for lost dreams and for the lost memories we will never get to make. We grieve for all the 'never going to happen now's and all the hopes we have that turn to dust.

Grief is as odd as it is individualised. This book is my version of grief and yours will be different; it's unique to you and how you feel and then process it all. But unique is not what the brain wants to hear after someone dies. "Somebody please save me from this," is a more likely reaction.

I was once a professional life coach, so I feel extremely qualified to say this: I would warn you about the peril of positivity at this time. People around you try and make everything OK, but they can't unless they actually can bring back the dead. When grieving you don't have to have your 'chin up' or 'be positive'; it's not needed for you to 'be brave' or have the very English (stupid) stiff upper lip.

"What doesn't kill you makes you stronger." Utter bullshit!

"God only gives you what you can handle." Oh, please!

People don't understand that all those well-used softeners feel more like knives at this time. Don't feel you have to be positive or fake happy or fake OK; be honest with yourself and those around you. Grief isn't the mumps; it isn't contagious. And if people around you can't handle your sadness, then they can, and will, stay away. This is when you find out how many of the people around you are willing to 'give' without gain.

My advice to any newly bereaved person is, don't try and hurry grieving. Your boss at work may have given you the standardised two weeks off to get over Mum, but it doesn't mean you will. Take all the time you need. It's a hugely strange time in your life and I think it's best that it's honoured. Take it slow and don't be too hard on yourself. In truth you're not yourself at the minute and may not feel back to normal for a long time, if ever.

Don't expect to 'get better' any time soon, but equally, you're not sick. You are completely out of sorts and out of whack, but you're not ill. Grieving is a natural response to losing a valued and adored loved one. In short, it fucking hurts.

I found that my mind played some extremely nasty tricks on me after losing Brett. Throughout the initial days, weeks and months after Brett's death, my mind went into overdrive and kept thinking, and repeating, the weirdest things such as: all the things that Brett was going to miss, the events, the birthdays, the weddings, the meals out, the holidays. My mind frantically role-played these events with Brett missing and decided it was going to be just awful and too sad for words. My mind kept going off at a tangent too, sometimes about completely non-related panics regarding the deaths of people who were still alive and well. I kept seeing disasters and things going wrong everywhere, and it just added to the overall traumatised feelings I was experiencing.

Everything in life seemed unstable, unsafe, risky and unbalanced. Then, as if the role-playing movies in my mind weren't enough, it threw into the sad soup things like, just what I thought of Brett as a person, how much I love him, then there was his love for me, the wonderful things he'd said to me.

It role-played us hugging each other then added, with all the dramatic power of a Morgan Freeman voiceover, "You'll never hug each other again," and that then would trigger another spiral down into the depths of despair. My mind was my biggest enemy; it wouldn't let me sleep or escape the constant stream of sad thoughts. Just getting the mind to shut up for a small amount of time became my biggest goal. Watching TV was useless, as I couldn't concentrate on anything. I drank yet never managed to get drunk and it still didn't help me sleep (I know 'they' say it actually makes it harder).

Initially, I couldn't detach from the sad train for even a moment. Eventually, the initial roaring, panicky feelings started to calm a little and became something deeper. It was a cold, sombre, painful feeling that, for me, has never really gone. And then came anger. Anger was, and is, a huge part of my personal grieving, which is why it has its own chapter.

I'm not saying this to scare anyone; it's simply what happened to me. Those times felt awful, but they eventually settled down a bit and I found some techniques which were very useful. Firstly, I think it's important to try and get a little respite from your mind and its constant stream of thoughts. As we know, thoughts equal feelings, and when grieving, those feelings are hideously powerful and, obviously, mostly always sad. You can be sitting having a coffee without particularly feeling anything and your mind will dump a thought that can send you reeling into sadness, but it doesn't have to constantly be that way.

I would interrupt my mind when it was in full throttle, playing back something I particularly didn't wish to see again, such as Brett's actual death; I would say in my mind in a loud voice, *NO, excuse me! NO.*

It was my way of trying to start to take a bit of control back.

Your mind will do what it wants to, if left to its own devices, but you can actually control it. You don't have to believe every thought it tells you either. I started to question and often told myself not to be so silly when some extremely farfetched scenario started being played out. Question your mind and tell it to shut up whenever you want.

Try and find the silence in between the thoughts and then try to lengthen the gap. It's called mindfulness, and there is a lot of information around on it.

There are two authors who are particularly useful in the field of quietening the mind. The first one is Mark Williams. His book, *Mindfulness, A Practical Guide to Finding Peace in a Frantic World*, includes a useful CD.

The second author I recommend is Eckhart Tolle. He has many books and programmes available. He teaches how to be the observer of the talker (which is the mind) and the constant tapes it plays. Eckhart's teachings show you how to actually watch and catch your mind as it speaks and how it sends your thoughts. The ultimate goal is to have no thoughts at all, which is a definite challenge. Initially, it feels a bit weird, but I find it extremely useful and quite soothing.

I highly recommend you look them up, or not, if it doesn't appeal to you. It's your bereavement path. Meditation can also soothe an overactive mind effectively, and there are even apps for it now. Some people read or listen to music – whatever works for you.

My mind continued to try and often succeeded in being a sneaky little snake by the way it made the grief subtly invade my very being. When I was able to sleep, I'd have severe nightmares that nearly caused me to wet the bed, or in direct contrast, I'd have terrible insomnia. I spent hours staring at the bedroom ceiling, wishing for morning. Isn't it odd that the morning light makes things seem a little bit better? I never fussed about the nightmares or the insomnia; I just accepted it was part of the process. Most of the physical effects eventually do go, although I still suffer from insomnia and bad nightmares on occasions.

Physical ailments started popping up; my husband had a terrible pain in his upper back which appeared out of nowhere about a week after Brett's funeral. He was in agony, so he went and saw a doctor, who told him it was 'just grief'. Needless to say, my husband thought the doctor was an absolute idiot. Grief? How could it be grief? The pain was real, it was physical. Kev took some of the painkillers prescribed to begin with but then just lived with the pain, which, incidentally, did go away all on its own about eight to ten weeks later, just as the doctor said it would.

I had to go and see a doctor less than a week after my Brett died; I needed an asthma inhaler as I'd failed to remember to put in my re-order in time and I wasn't allowed do a telephone repeat, so I had had to go and see a doctor in person – just what I didn't want to do. I walked into his office and immediately he said, "Ahh, I know why you're here, you need some help with your grief," as he reached for his prescription pad. I was horrified, and explained I just needed an inhaler and left quickly. It had been less than a week – why would I be reaching for the pills and why would he encourage it? I was, and still am, very sad my little boy is dead (little boy, aged eighteen and height 5'11"). Tablets won't bring him back. When someone dies, you are sad and unhappy and maybe scared, but you're not sick. Society needs to sod off with its pill-giving for everything

'Take away the pain' is the general attitude, but what is the real cost? Grieving isn't nice, but I don't see that turning yourself into a drug-filled zombie is the solution either.

Although, if you feel you want tablets, then have them. It's completely your choice; only you know how you feel. As long as it is *you* who wants the tablets and not the people around you or what the doctor thinks is best for you.

Death can't be cured and neither can the effects of someone's death on us; there are no quick fixes. People say it's the price you pay for loving someone. People generally just talk *a lot* around the bereaved; my advice is, take what you like and throw the rest away.

People talk about 'working through your grief'; again, I think that's utter crap. Grief works at its own speed, and anyway, why do people act like grief is a job to be done like mowing the lawn? Just get through those stages people talk about and at the end you're happy and grieving is over! I call bullshit on that one. *But*, again, if that's what you want to do, then do it. There are grief courses and counselling readily available if that's what you decide to try.

It's often said that death and grieving make you taste your own mortality and that it finally dawns on you that you are going to die someday, which might spark strong internal dialogue and/or even panic.

It didn't happen like that for me. I made peace with the idea of death years ago; I have never felt immortal. I've always known that I'm born, I'm here, then I will die. I always thought of it like we all have an invisible 'sell-by date' on the back of our heads that we can't see but that we are closing in on every day.

I don't fear death because I'm either going to be with my son again whilst waiting for the rest of the family to return home too, or I will find out I am completely wrong about the whole business, that there isn't life after death and there's actually nothing after we die. But I'm not worried, as I'll be dead, so it won't bother me. I won't even have time to think, *I was wrong... hey ho.*

Grief is so weird it's almost abstract, some days I look at my son's pictures that adorn every wall of this house and I feel filled with pure love; my heart swells with pride; I smile and blow him a kiss and tell him I love him.

Then other days, I look at my son's pictures that adorn every wall of this house and my heart feels like it will explode with pain. Anger rises from deep within me and I feel like ripping the pictures down off the wall as his beautiful vision is way too painful for me to even look at.

All those different thoughts I have, they really do drive me crazy... What could have been? What fun we had, how I love you, Brett. It's not as if every day is different whilst grieving a loved one; it can be different every hour.

I feel so guilty being here. I shouldn't be alive whilst my son is dead.

Mothers die before their children – that's the law; it's the universal Mummy Oath.

You can't mess up the circle of life; it's just not right.

Everyone silently agrees too, which is why, subsequently, there were no rules for us. People really don't know what to say to parents of a dead child. If you've spent your life adhering to all the rules society has on every subject, and there are many rules, can you imagine how weird it feels when suddenly none of them are applied to you?

We literally have a get-out-of-jail card; nobody expects anything from us. We can behave as we wish because no one knows how to advise grieving parents and they won't dare tell us off for our bad or strange behaviour because our situation seems to just genuinely terrify people. We have the ultimate horror of losing a child and therefore we are even more outcast than normal grieving people, and that's saying something.

In the beginning people avoided us like the plague. I noticed in the area where we used to live, people would start to come out of their house as I was walking past, only for them to see me, turn and walk back inside. God forbid they should speak to me. It was the same in the supermarket; initially I thought I was seeing spirits, as these strange apparitions were darting about quickly and I could only just catch them out of the corner of my eye. Unfortunately, I soon discovered that they weren't angels or mystical spirits sent to care for and love me. No! They were stupid people I once knew, who, upon seeing me, ran down the first aisle possible to get out of the way.

The funniest case of the 'grieving invisibility cloak' was when an old friend from my past life (pre-poorly son) actually stood in a lift right next to me, as the lift was so full, and *still* didn't acknowledge me. The girl whom I'd originally gone shopping with that day was on the opposite side of the lift and said to me, "What are you laughing at?" She didn't know this 'old friend' of mine who was stood right next to me and was concerned that I was in a state of giggles in a lift full of strangers, so she thought I had finally lost it. I had even tried to talk to the old friend next to me and I had said, "Hello," but she decided in that very instant that she had a phone call on her mobile and got busy chatting. I didn't hear the mobile phone ring nor could I hear even the faintest sound of anyone talking back to her, and I was very close so I think I would have heard something. I could have been wrong, but I doubt it, so in that instant I started laughing because I couldn't believe she was so afraid to talk to me because I was (and still am) grieving.

What did she think I was going to do? Burst into hysterical tears because she had taken the courage to whisper, "Hello, Sarah."

Was I going to fall onto the floor, grabbing at her legs whilst screaming and sobbing, "He's gone, he's gone, my baby's gone"?

No, you prat! I would have said, "Hello," back, followed by, "How are you?"

Even then, I wasn't angry at that old friend; I just felt sorry for her inability to function around death.

It's really quite insulting that our fellow human beings can't cope with the fact of life that everyone will experience, and that is the death of a loved one. Everyone – regardless of their ethnicity, religion, race, gender, wealth – will feel the loss of a loved one at least once in their lives.

I was lucky enough (or I guess it's unlucky) to be surrounded by other grieving families who had gone through very similar experiences and lost their precious children too. The hospital admits it had a 'couple of bad years' – a couple of bad years for them means a huge group of broken families. Some of the families had lost their children a few months prior to us and some were to follow after.

Even though we were all grieving our children who had passed because of cancer, we still didn't grieve in the same way. I was very often surrounded by other grieving mothers who were expressing their anger at the hospital, family, people around them, God, anyone, yet I felt no anger myself for months. I realise now that at that time it was because I couldn't feel anything, nothing but a cold, dark ache that permeated from the very bottom of my soul. (The anger did come and stayed, but more about that later in its own chapter.)

After Brett died, I found the basic physical aspects of day-to-day life, that changed so suddenly, was very hard to cope with too.

I had nothing to do.

I had cared for Brett physically, mentally and emotionally his whole life but exceptionally closely during the five years that led up to his death. The cancer years were intolerable and completely ruined any life we had as a family, yet we still obviously had family routines, like where we all sat in the living room or round the dinner table – 'our chairs and places', as it were. It was so weird being this new family of three. Empty chairs and new spaces had popped up, and it was just horrible.

One Sunday, dinner was very late (or, if memory serves me correctly, probably became a takeaway). I had gone about my business that Sunday quite automatically and absentmindedly when I suddenly noticed I'd set the dinner table for the four of us. When I realised what I'd done I was devastated. I could do nothing, as I found I couldn't move. I was paralysed with the realisation that we weren't a four anymore. The truth of the situation seemed to hit me all at once. I stood and stared at that dinner table for what seemed like hours.

Kev later found me just sitting on the kitchen floor. I was sitting, silently hugging the newly spare plate whilst the dinner burnt away in the oven. Such is loss.

I used to sometimes imagine Brett was just upstairs playing his Xbox. It was a nice fantasy. It soothed my soul and not much was able to do that. I desperately wanted soothing from my pain and one of the worst aspects of losing Brett was the realisation that no one or nothing could or would ever be able to soothe the pain within me again. I knew I would *never* get over his death nor be able to just 'move on'. The mere suggestion of 'moving on' made me furious.

People – kind-hearted, well-meaning people – want you to move on and not look back. They said things like, "It's what Brett would have wanted," and my head screams (shortly followed sometimes by my mouth, depending on how I'm feeling that day), *How the fuck would you know what Brett would have wanted? You didn't know him. You may have visited the hospital once in a blue moon, but that doesn't make you qualified to be able to say you knew him.*

How can people say move on? Move on from what, anyway? What the hell does moving on even mean in this context?

Move on from the memories? The pain? Or the sheer existence of your lost child? Basically, it's just a well-spun society catchphrase that surfaces in the brain when you're faced with a person who's grieving.

God forbid independent thinking. No! Just say the generic, allegedly useful statement.

People behave like sheep when they're faced with someone who's lost a loved one: *Oh, yes, I know what should be said here!* "You need to move on." Their brain then says, if met by resistance from said grieving person, just add, "It's what [insert name] would have wanted." Baaaa.

If that fails, there's always the other well-used soother statement: "Time heals," but remember if using this statement, please don't forget to put your head to one side in the standard alleged sympathy pose.

Sorry people, no! You're wrong again – time doesn't heal; time fades the oh-so-precious memories that I am so desperate to cling on to.

I remember being in the supermarket buying my daughter some chocolate for her school lunchbox and I literally went into a huge panic because I thought I couldn't remember what Brett's favourite chocolate was. My eyes frantically scanned the shelves with my mind screaming, *Was it this one? No, was it that one? No. Oh my God, I can't remember what chocolate my own son liked. I'm losing him; I'm losing the memories.* My heart was racing and I was probably heading for a full-blown panic attack when, luckily, I realised I had my mobile phone, so I called my daughter who calmed me down with, "He liked this one, he liked that one, it's OK, calm down, you're OK, breathe."

Do you really think I want to hear that time heals? And again, heals what exactly? The pain? Does any parent really think they will be able to heal the pain after losing their child? I used to say to people, "Look at your child or children, pick one and imagine them dead – reckon you'd get over it?" The look of sheer horror that appeared on their faces was normally enough for me to see they even slightly got what I was saying, and I say slightly because you can't ever imagine what it's like to lose a child. Your mind would never allow you to fall into that abyss unless it actually happens to you.

Too good for this Earth.

God only takes the best.

Too beautiful and special for this place.

God wanted his angel back.

If you do say these to a parent who's grieving their child, my advice is to stand back quickly straight after saying it. You may get a smack on the nose. What seems like a good idea and a calming, flattering statement to you is often deeply offensive to the parent.

In my case, I didn't want to hear my son Brett was an angel, and I didn't care that God wanted him back. God was a selfish bastard; I wanted my son safe in my loving arms, not in some place that none of us can even confirm exists.

When someone dies, the people around you all spout off about heaven like it's somewhere commonly travelled to, like Florida, and they were there only last week. The truth about heaven is that we're only going to know for sure it even exists when it's our time to go there. Which then leaves your loved one potentially either in a wondrous paradise or all alone, out in the cold and dark nothingness, depending on which level of grey grief day you're experiencing.

People think they can understand and empathise, but they can't; they truly can't. So very often people will say to a grieving parent, "I know how you feel, I've lost a neighbour/aunty/dog," which makes you stare at them in utter disbelief and think, *So what?! Do you really think that's a fair comparison?*

Also, personally, I don't care how you feel at this moment in time; it's about me, not you. Stop downplaying my emotions to make yourself feel better.

"I got over the death of my mother very quickly and was back at work within the week." So bloody what?! What do you want, a medal?

Don't let people tell you how you should be feeling because that's how they felt or, even more appallingly, how they think they would feel in a similar circumstance.

In our case, I feel even the loss of a parent to some extent isn't a fair comparison because parents are supposed to die before you. It's the circle of life. To watch the child that you adore, that you brought into this world, suffer so horribly in pain and agony for years, then die in front of your very eyes, I feel is virtually without comparison in the world in which we live today.

But that's the point, that's the very point I'm trying to make. We've got to stop comparing, assessing and trying to put people in categories.

You could be devastated that your 108-year-old father has died. You could feel your pain is 'virtually without comparison in the world in which we live today', and you would be right. Because it's your pain, and no one should feel the need to validate their personal experience and feelings. Don't get drawn into the 'it's worse for me than you' games.

Sometimes the more someone tries to understand you, the more they are trying to pigeonhole you and your experience. Sweeping generalisations are insulting at best and damaging at worst. How did we end up with this one-size-fits-all society? Especially when there are so many people on the planet.

I definitely don't fit into the standard one-size-fits-all grieving model (which doesn't even exist in my opinion), so that's left me and a lot of my cancer family friends up a certain creek without a paddle. Or another way of saying it is 'alone and support-less'.

It's almost as if I could cope better if he'd never existed. Would you want to feel that way about your child? I hope not, and me neither.

The truth is, no one actually fits the standard grieving model because people are not standard; they're individual. Also, I did not mean to offer any disrespect to people who are a terrible sad mess over losing their neighbour/aunty/dog; my point was no one should have their emotions downplayed or pigeonholed, because it's seriously insulting.

After all that being said, the strange thing is, if I was the one who died I would actually want everyone to go about their business unperturbed and get over me quickly. I would hate to think of my family crying and not getting on with their lives. I wouldn't want people to mourn me forever, but I didn't die, and it's not that easy to forget someone who imprinted so beautifully on your heart like Brett did.

And anyway, I am pretty awesome, and I would leave a large hole in my loved ones' lives. (What? That's not arrogant, I'm just being honest, ha, ha.)

Brett will always be missed; it's the missing that is the biggest hurt. I've lost today and all our tomorrows. There is always going to be an empty chair, at birthdays, Christmas, any celebrations, Poppy's wedding – oh my God! I actually dread it already. I am condemned to never fully enjoy anything the way I could have if Brett had survived. That's a really depressing thing to think, but it's the truth as I see it. I adore my son and my daughter, but the fact that he's somewhere else unknown makes life unbearable. Most things said to soothe the grieving are so benign whilst the honest truth is left in the silence.

It is utterly heart-breaking to know you'll never see your loved one here again. It is just so inherently sad.

Wherever you are with regards to bereavement, whether recently bereaved or if it was thirty years ago, I send you my heartfelt love and I want you to know that you are not alone. Grieving can be temporary or can become a major part of who you are. It doesn't matter. You're only grieving because you've lost someone you love, and I'm sure they love you too, wherever they are.

And just when the caterpillar thought the world was over, he became a beautiful butterfly...

Seriously?! What utter bollocks!

Chapter 5

Possessions, Porsches and Performance Reviews

A few months after Brett passed away, Poppy was struggling very deeply with his loss and decided she wanted to sleep in his bedroom to feel closer to him. I was dubious about it, as I didn't want her sleeping in a 'living, breathing shrine' to him, but I was so desperate to help her feel better, I decided to give it a go.

I know some grieving parents who find their child's room a place of comfort, a private haven that allows them to be at one with their child's memory and connect to their child's soul and the very essence of their being. Other grieving parents find their child's bedroom devastatingly torturous, an overpowering, ghost-like room which has become an empty, hollow vessel where once-thriving life existed. There are no right or wrongs between them. It is what it is, and the empty space represents different things at different times to different parents.

Going into Brett's room, for me, felt as though I was violating his private personal space. All his belongings were in that room, the room that he saw as his private teenage cave, where he could get away from us, his annoying family. It was a place where he could be alone quietly with his thoughts or scream aloud, laughing and shouting, whilst playing Xbox or PlayStation online with his friends. As Brett couldn't go out much due to his cancer treatments, he found online gaming with his school and fellow cancer friends as an invaluable way of staying close and connected to them. He loved hearing their gossip whilst they all played the same game together, and I loved hearing his jokey banter with them and his laughter. I miss his laughter so very much.

Brett's Xbox and PlayStation were the only things we hadn't touched until we moved house nearly three years after his death, and if we hadn't moved house I think they would have still been left where they were. They still had the last games in them that he was playing before he got very ill and died. His headset was still connected to the game's unit and his other favourite games of choice were still next to the machines. I used to dust the games unit, making sure I put everything back in the same place. It was odd to think that those games units that gave such fun and were used so much, were now just dusty, historic ornaments, symbols of much happier times.

Whilst preparing to move Poppy into Brett's room, I decided it was a great time to go through Brett's cupboards and drawers and pack everything away. Brett had left everything he owned to Poppy; he actually told her this to her face when he realised he only had a few days to live. It's a conversation I try not to think of because the vision of my two children holding hands, crying and saying all the things we never really ever say to each other: the pure, honest and deep 'I love you'; the 'I'll always be with you no matter what'; the 'we will be together again one day'...

No two children should have to say their goodbyes to each other and no parents should have to watch their children do it. We had stood by helpless, unable to offer any real comfort whilst our 'babies' broke their hearts with each other during what was going to be one of their last times on this Earth together. I think saying goodbye is over-rated. I don't believe in goodbye and told my children this at that time and many times since. It's not goodbye; it's just see you later, because our souls carry on and love is eternal.

Before going back to the original story, by the way, I feel there is no 'good time' to go through a deceased person's treasured belongings and it should only be done when the living person is ready. Having said that, often we are not allowed the luxury of time in which to feel ready. If the deceased lived in a rented place, like both my nans did, you have only a very short amount of time allowed to clear everything out. It's very heartless, really, as you have to sort through everything, every drawer, every cupboard – take what you want and get rid of the rest as quickly as possible.

It's a horribly draining and deeply emotional rollercoaster, plus I always feel like a burglar, a stranger pillaging through someone else's possessions, their 'treasures' with the sole purpose of deciding what I think is of value and what isn't, and by value I don't necessarily mean financially valuable. It's a wretched time, and I truly feel for anyone who has had to clear away another loved one's lifelong possessions they've gathered.

I had the arduous task of helping my husband clear his mother and father's huge three-bedroom home when they passed. He was their only child, so the task lay firmly at his feet. I was only a daughter-in-law, yet I had to empty my mother-in-law's most private drawers and units. Some of the things she obviously felt were incredible special to her were just placed in rubbish bags. Brett was alive at the time and in remission from his cancer, so he and Poppy came to the house to choose some items to remember their nanna and grandad by. Brett chose some old, battered, metal toy cars and a box of old pencils; Poppy chose a few of her favourite Nanna scarfs and an old tin box full of buttons. There were a lot of far more 'expensive' items in that crammed pack house, but our children chose mementos which were special to them; it was very sweet and innocent and the true meaning of keeping a few of our loved ones' treasures.

Going through Brett's possessions was easier in the respect that we weren't throwing any of it away. Actually, quite the reverse: we packed everything carefully into suitcases. But it was harder in the fact that he was my baby boy and finding some of the things he felt were 'treasures' was deeply distressing. Poppy and I spent a whole day going through his room; we laughed and we cried a lot! I gasped at finding different sweet and meaningful treasures he'd saved such as a tiny card I'd sent him telling him how much I loved him and how I was so proud of him. He had tutted and rolled his eyes at the time when he opened it, so to find it safely tucked away was so heart-warming. There were ticket stubs from the football games he had been to and a couple of music concerts. He had hidden some of the soft toys Poppy had bought him. We thought he hadn't kept them, but he had – turns out he was a real sweet little softie.

He had kept the cinema ticket stub from when he and my husband had gone to see the James Bond *Skyfall* movie together. Poppy put the ticket stub to one side and gave it to my husband in one of Brett's old wallets as a Father's Day present. It broke his heart – "Happy Father's Day, you're gonna cry!" – but it remains one of his favourite presents ever. He was so touched knowing that that cinema trip they had taken together had impressed on Brett enough for him to treasure the ticket.

Brett had a whole cupboard full of 'bottom drawer stuff', such as new mugs, salt and pepper pots, and general household things ready for when he was well enough to move out and live with his best friend as they had always planned to do. They are still in a box, safe and sound. Why? I don't know. Why don't I take them out and use them? No, never. What if one broke? In a box is safer, but they are definitely not being saved for any fun purpose now.

Poppy kept all Brett's possessions on the top of the cupboards in his room just where they were and his pictures all on the walls so, in essence, the room looked just the same. It turned out that she wasn't happier in his room, but at least she tried. There are no shortcuts to feeling better after losing someone you adore. But you have to try, and that was a brave move on her part. She was, and is, heartbroken. The brother that she fought with constantly, like normal siblings, and who she thought would be around to annoy her forever, was gone, and she finds it soul-destroying. She was desperate to have him back, but she had to come to terms with the fact that it wasn't to be.

After we'd sorted Brett's 'treasures', it made me think about all the stuff we had accumulated over the years. Our three-bedroom house was packed full of stuff. We had boxes in the loft space; our garage had so much stuff in it we couldn't have got our car in it even if we had wanted to. We didn't really know what any of it was, let alone if any of it was wanted or loved. Over the course of the next few months, we threw ourselves into clearing out. It was not only a useful distraction from our pain but my first real insight to how Brett's death had changed me as a person. I wanted to travel light for the rest of my life and that kind of became my mantra.

I wasn't crazily materialistic before Brett got cancer; I had always preferred spending any spare money on holidays and days out instead of excessive shoes and handbags. But even so, there was more stuff than we would ever need. We had always struggled financially; we lived in the 'just getting by' bracket like millions of others, but we were very grateful for what we had. We had both been brought up to look after things well, so there was lots of perfectly preserved stuff that we no longer needed or wanted. Nearly every toy the kids had ever had was still in prime condition. I was astonished at the sheer volume of crap that appeared on the opening of each box, drawer and cupboard. We sorted the stuff repeatedly into piles: rubbish, charity and sellable. I started selling what I could.

Brett's cancer journey had left us financially screwed, so every little helped. It's not even as if we have to pay for cancer treatment in England, as we have the National Health Service, but we couldn't cope with the loss of both of our wages over the years. I instantly lost my wages after Brett was diagnosed and Kev lost a lot of his when he couldn't attend work when Brett was desperately ill (which in Brett's case was often). Then add on the expenses of living in a hospital. The ill child gets food, but the parent doesn't, which translates to – if I never see a packaged sandwich again in my life it will be too soon. I lived off chocolate, biscuits and crisps because they were easy and grabbable. I didn't want to leave Brett's side and go out and get a meal – that would have been too selfish. Going back and forth to the hospital cost us a minimum of £70 in petrol each week. The mortgage still had to be paid and all the bills – they don't care if someone has cancer.

The financial losses we accrued will never be replaced; it doesn't matter compared to losing Brett, but it was another knife in the back. As a family we were broke and broken.

When we were clearing out the house, I found the really important valuables appeared in the form of Brett and Poppy's old school books and drawings I'd saved over the years. We found Poppy and Brett's first few pairs of tiny shoes, some baby clothes, their drinking cups and plastic food plates with their favourite characters on them. These were worth their weight in gold to me. The rest of the stuff meant nothing to me. I sold my jewellery to try and help with our perpetual overdraft at the bank. We even sold both our weddings rings. People around us were shocked, but we didn't care. We truly didn't care about 'things' or 'stuff' anymore.

People matter, not things. Something that can help you recall a lovely memory of your loved ones is a true treasure; anything else is just needless clutter in my eyes now. If I was to suddenly die, I hated to think of my husband and my daughter clearing out my private drawers and cupboards. I was determined to get my house in order and clear the crap out myself.

I have burnt reams of useless paperwork such as old educational courses that I had completed, a million old bank statements that I had kept for years 'just in case I needed them'. I even went through my computer and all the random memory sticks I found. I sorted all the photographs, the physical ones and the ones on the computer; and all the random crappy documents I'd kept 'just in case' were deleted too.

My travelling light mantra, I came to realise, meant much more than just physical items around the home. I was wrangling with so many deep questions after Brett died: why did he die now, after over five years of fighting? If there is a God, why would he have made Brett suffer so horribly for so long and *then* take him anyway? What had I done wrong to deserve my child being taken away from me? What is this damn mean evil life all about anyway? What's the point to this life? Is this instead hell maybe, hell on Earth?

All my questions remain unanswered. But the house was tidy.

I then went on to realise that travelling light also meant letting go of the heavy burdens of guilt, remorse and shame I was carrying over the millions of different and very difficult choices I had had to make during Brett's cancer treatments and ultimately, the guilt of not being able to save my son from dying.

I had guilt over things such as when I had told him off when he was a small child. I was a bit of a strict parent. I believed in good manners and behaviours – I still do, but I guess my deepest, darkest regrets and almost shame is the way I wasted my precious time with my son and daughter. I was always busy. I was always organising something, planning something, doing something for a better, brighter future for us. I stayed at home in the day, worked at night after my husband came home from his work, and I also studied various courses to try and improve myself, my job prospects and, therefore, our quality of life. I so wish I could go back and tell that younger me to stop, just stop, and enjoy that precious, sacred time with my children.

I did improve my job prospects and that in turn lead to me being out of the home more and more. My career was growing and so were our finances, so everybody was happy, right? Wrong, my son later told me during one of our million heart-to-heart conversations in the hospital that he missed me terribly and would much rather me be home than working. And the money I made that bought us more holidays and him new stuff, he would have gladly given up because I was permanently stressed and always busy.

Sadly, it's true that I was stressed, overworked, tired. I fell foul of wanting 'it all', but I now realise, you can't have it all; it's an exhausting myth and you seem to end up with nothing – nothing of any true value, anyway. I was never in the 'now'; I was never 'present'. I lived in my mind, constantly going over my 'to-do' lists.

I was always working or thinking of work that I had to do; I was always cleaning or thinking about what needed cleaning next; I rushed around shopping and tried to prepare healthy, nutritious, home-cooked food, chop, chop, chop, chop – the food preparation took ages. I was always busy, whatever the reason. Basically, I was never 'present'. I may have been there physically, but I certainly wasn't there mentally – such a waste of what was going to be the best time of my life.

Travelling light into the future meant that I had to let go of my personal remorse for all my errors in life. That was way harder than clearing some old physical junk out. My mental junk is sneaky and slips back in when I think I have dealt with it and let it go. I think in times like these you have to just say to yourself, *I really did do what I thought was the best at that time, with the knowledge I had. I really was trying to get things going for the good of the whole family. When you know better, you do better, and I did what I thought was right then.*

Say it again, say it again. I repeat it, but I'm still not sure I really believe it yet. *When I knew better, I did better. I did what I thought was for the best. No one sets out to be a failure.* Say it again, Sarah.

The curse of the 'should have's, 'would have's, 'could have's and 'what if's after someone dies is mind-blowing. I wonder if anyone actually escapes the terror of their own personal performance review after a loved one dies? I wonder if people really do exist who don't question what they did or didn't do and whether they thought they were right or wrong, or did enough?

From what I know personally and from the grieving families around me, I've never yet met anyone who has thought they couldn't have done any better; most live in abject hell, questioning and blaming themselves over and over again.

In my case, the bottom line is, parents are supposed to protect their offspring and no matter what kind-hearted people say around them to soothe their frayed nerves, most grieving parents feel instinctively on some level that they have failed, and I am certainly no exception to that rule.

Brett's cancer created a number of deep personal changes for me.

Firstly, my career that I'd worked so hard on building disappeared overnight upon his diagnosis, and I couldn't have cared less.

Secondly, the value I placed on the future 'better times' vanished because the future was wobbly for a long while, then became without Brett so could never again 'be better'.

Thirdly, I learnt the true price of 'things'. I really do think that in this modern society we behave like a bunch of idiots because we place more value on money, possessions and 'stuff' than we do on spending time together and loving and caring for each other. Inanimate objects, figures in a bank account, the latest 'must-have' car, clothes, homes, jewellery all seem to matter the most. But they don't matter; it's a fake and plastic existence. When you're on your deathbed or, worse, sitting next to your child's deathbed, you are really not going to think, *Yeah, it's all been worthwhile. My son's dying, we could have done more together, but at least I have a Rolex watch.*

I think most of the things in life that the majority of people work and strive for are actually hollow and soulless. I did too once, but when you know better, you do better.

My personal performance review is: I should have slowed down and enjoyed it more. I would love to go back and change it all if it was possible, and I definitely would have/could have/should have done it all so much better.

(Blimey, it sounds very like my old school report.)

Chapter 6

Religion vs Spirituality – for Shits and Giggles

I always thought that death probably wasn't so much of a catastrophe for people who had a strong faith in their chosen religion. If you follow a religion, the thinking and wondering is sort of done for you, and I always thought what a relief that must be. Some of the other cancer families had a strong religious faith and I was a bit jealous that they had their God who was going to look after them and I thought maybe if I had a strong religion that I would have a God looking after Brett too. I started to wonder if it was actually my fault Brett was suffering as I had no strong faith.

I came to discover that the families with even the strongest religious beliefs weren't always as confident and sorted out as I had imagined, and often the cancer diagnosis of their child had sparked a deep internal assessment of whether they truly did 'believe' what their religion quoted or not.

Some parents even completely turned their backs on their faith when their children died as they were so enraged that their 'God' would do this to them and take their child. I felt that that was somehow sadder than the people who had no strong beliefs either way. For a person to lose their child and their religion, simultaneously, to let go of their hardcore beliefs and faith, somehow highlighted the depths of the devastating extent of the loss I was experiencing too. It made me feel not so alone.

I was brought up by my parents whose religion by birth was Church of England, which is a Christian faith. I wasn't heavily indoctrinated into the religion and I wasn't actually christened until I was twenty years old, and that was by my own choice because I wished to be a godmother to my nephew. I liked the beliefs that the religion upheld and the people at the church seemed very friendly, but my knowledge of the complete religion was a little woolly and maybe sometimes verged a bit on the sceptical side.

My mother and father believed that my brothers and I should go and find our own religion, if we wished, and that it was wrong for them to insist that we automatically believe in the religion that they had been brought up with. My parents did give us strong moral values which I believe transcends all religions, but they felt that questioning was healthy and solid beliefs were formed after serious thought and discussion.

My father's work involved travelling, so I was very lucky to live in different countries and experience different cultures whilst growing up. Over the years we discussed all sorts of religions and what was at their heart. I attended many different faith churches and I experienced a lot of the different religions, but one single faith never stood out to me. I eventually chose a path more spiritual. I strongly believe that people should be allowed to believe whatever they wish, as long as they equally allow others with different views to do the same and live in peace.

I feel my beliefs are really quite simple. I believe in love, peace and respecting each other. I do believe there is an afterlife and that our soul goes on. I think we are a family in the afterlife as well as down here. I believe there is a higher power, but I'm not sure what that power is. The rest is shaky.

I talk to God sometimes, but mostly I shout at him. I always felt there was a God and that he was a good, loving person or entity, but not now. If I did believe in him, I'd be incredibly mad with him; he took my son away from me and I can't see what I did to deserve such an evil punishment.

I was so relieved the first time I came across someone else questioning their religious beliefs. It was early on just after Brett's cancer diagnosis. We were on a ward of four – four children with cancer, which meant a little ward with barely any walking space between the beds, whilst each bed had a whole family around them. It was tightly packed, but it just meant that we got to know each other more quickly and it was extremely valuable to get talking to other families who were going through the same horror.

On the ward there was an Asian family who closed the curtains around their child's bed at various times in the day to pray. The rest of us on the ward tried to stay quiet when they did this so they could have their private family prayer time together. I was really quite envious of them, as I wished I had a strong religious faith to believe in too. I was busy calling God every name imaginable every time I left the hospital to drive home and back again.

My dad had bought me a gold cross to wear when Brett got diagnosed; he himself has always worn a silver St Christopher around his neck. St Christopher was the patron saint of travellers and he believed it bought him great luck. He had bought Brett a St Christopher to wear too. I didn't know if I believed in God back then and thought if he did exist, why was he being such a bastard? But I didn't want to have a debate with my dad and thought maybe it would bring luck, who knew?

Anything is worth a go, I'd thought.

I actually felt bad and guilty about this decision too; I was wearing a cross whilst swearing at God any chance I got. *You crazy, stupid woman*, my mind raged.

One evening the Asian dad was washing his hands at the sink, which happened to be by Brett's bed. We smiled at each other and, on seeing the cross around my neck, he asked me, "So are you a Christian?" I was a bit taken aback by his question and especially when I replied, "Yes, I think so."

Am I? my mind screamed. *That's news to me.*

He went on to tell me in a whispered voice that his little boy's cancer had relapsed and he now needed extremely severe treatment, and even then, it didn't look good for the child; hope was fading. He told me how he and his wife secretly questioned their God and their religion as a whole but couldn't say anything out loud because their two extended families would be horrified at them for even having those thoughts. I told him how I had just acquired my new cross and that it was being worn in a sad desperation to appease a God who probably knew I doubted him, even though I was wearing it. I was hoping God would forgive me and still look after Brett. At the end of our conversation the dad stood up and said, "Well, how about I pray for Brett and you pray for my child? So we can sort of hedge our bets, as it were." I smiled and readily agreed. Hedge our bets – yes, why not? Two gods might be better than one.

To lots of religious people, that's a probably an incredibly offensive story, but it's true, and to me it was a golden moment. I was so sure that that family had a handle on their beliefs and religion, but it just showed me that something like your child getting cancer can shock you to your core. I wasn't the only one confused, questioning everything and angry at God. There is an unspoken expectation for gods of any faith, that they should protect the children at the very least.

I used to believe in a god. I believed he was like an old, bearded man who was kind and would save you from anything nasty if he felt you were good enough and if you were a nice person. You needed to behave well and not be mean or evil. You had to be kind of spirit and have a charitable heart. You needed to be generous and thank him for all your blessings which were plentiful. He was a good God and he would grace you if you behaved. I realise now how laughable it sounds. I actually sound about six years old, all sweet, innocent and naive.

The day I witnessed a tiny new-born baby being rushed into the cancer ward in an incubator for emergency cancer treatment, that inner six-year-old innocent child dissolved in horror and I can sadly say that after everything I've witnessed, I do not believe in God. In my diaries across the years they are filled with chats to him, prayers and appreciations. I thought he was my friend.

I think it's more accurate to say God stopped believing in me way before I gave up on him.

Some people turn to religion when the shit hits the fan, or the diagnosis happens, but I think it's too late then. Isn't that like trying to get car insurance after the car crash? People pray when everything else has failed, but they pray with panic. Their hearts and minds are filled with words of begging to appease a God who could save them if he wanted to. I don't think they really believe in him but are engulfed by doubt and fear. If God exists, surely a relationship that begins with the performance-based emphasis on him, must be a little irritating to him?

God you must perform your magic then I will believe in you.

To be fair, though, when Brett was diagnosed with cancer, I tried everything. I prayed, I begged, I pleaded, and when that didn't work, I shouted and cursed. I wished so hard that if we did have any magic inside of us, I would have used all my life's fairy dust on Brett and I'd be now left with an empty jar.

I cannot believe in a God that controls this planet and everything that goes on in it. That means God allows wars to rage, people to die from starvation and lack of clean water (in this day and age, I mean, please!), and children can be raped by healthy paedophiles. Children are allowed to be extremely sick with cancer and endure unimaginable pain and suffering before they finally die. No loving, caring God would allow that to happen, surely?

Many say that God has given us free will with our lives here. So, to play devil's advocate – it's our free will which controls the day-to-day running of the show of life (which strikes me as convenient) and a lot of people would argue that my examples are manmade problems. Wars, paedophiles, starving countries could all be potentially solved by the women and men on this planet.

OK! That might be true, but not child cancer, though; there's neither logic nor excuses for child cancer.

The lifestyle guidelines given to ensure you are less likely to get cancer don't apply to the children. They haven't smoked a pack of cigarettes a day, eaten loads of unhealthy junk food or drank themselves into a stupor every night for 40 years.

When I was pregnant, I took my vitamins, avoided all the banned foods like ice cream and pate, etc. I was a rule follower to the letter. My only sin I had was that I smoked a few cigarettes, but not in pregnancy and never in the house or car. I was the idiot who went down the bottom of the garden in the middle of winter for a quick puff (again, in England, that's quite a mean feat) Any and every rule given I followed, no questions asked, and I honoured the little life growing inside of me by trying to nourish it every step of the way. After Brett was born, he was fed the best food, taken out in the fresh air to play, had carefully selected 'safe' toys, the house was decorated in 'safe' paint – do I need to go on? I was the stereotypical rule-following mum.

The teenage cancer units were full of previously very healthy, sporty kids. Every kid we met had at least one sport they played, they weren't overweight (until the treatment started; then the moon face and fat stomach 'steroids look' was abound) and they all had nice, decent, over-the-top health-conscious, intelligent parents like us. It all made no sense at all.

All I could derive from it was they were all wrong. All the rules I had followed had been bullshit and for nothing. They had made no difference; the rule makers were wrong.

The people who spouted on endlessly about health and wellbeing were wrong. The studies, the facts, the 'scientist says'... were wrong. The walls of the child cancer units scream *bullshit* about every subject you have ever thought you knew anything about.

It was Christmas Day 2012 and Brett was in hospital in an isolation ward; he had been there since his bone marrow transplant in the November. I had just swapped over with my husband, Kev (we did twenty-four-hour shifts each at the hospital), so I had been able to see my daughter, Poppy, on Christmas morning, though we didn't open any presents; it really didn't feel like Christmas. Kev and Poppy were going for Christmas dinner at my parents. Kev didn't want to go as he was exhausted from being awake with Brett most of the night. Brett was so very poorly and Kev didn't feel like he could fake a smile any longer. But he knew it was good for Poppy. I was a little sad, as I wished we could all be together, but I just kept dreaming of next year, which would hopefully be better.

I was still smoking then. It was about 3pm and I went outside for a cigarette. I left the transplant ward knowing I would have to scrub up again to go back in, but I really needed a cigarette and Brett had finally fallen asleep, and as I didn't know when I'd next have the chance, I took it.

The transplant ward was part of the children's cancer ward. Even though it was Christmas Day, the ward was unusually very quiet and it had a weird, eerie feeling. It was a kind of heaviness which I quickly realised I knew what it meant. Sure enough, there was a large family gathered in the outside corridor, which I thought was great for me, as I should get let back into the ward easily enough, as normally I had to wait for a busy staff member to let me in (the ward doors were looked for safety, yet it made it feel more like a prison). I noticed the two single rooms on the ward were occupied; they were saved for the sickest children, and judging by the amount of family gathered, it wouldn't be too long for one of them.

After my cigarette I re-entered the ward only to be met by a woman screaming and the whole family crying. An elderly woman suddenly collapsed onto the floor; nurses ran to her aid. The little one had obviously just passed away. I walked by as quickly as I could; this wasn't a time to be a spectator and anyway, I couldn't stop, as I needed to get back to Brett. I had been around children dying many times before, but for some reason it seemed so much sadder and more poignant on Christmas Day. Little did I know that it would be us at home with our child dying the following year.

And the walls of the child cancer ward screamed again, "A god? *Bullshit!*"

It really drives me crazy when people say (especially celebrities during interviews on TV) that it was due to 'the grace of God' that their child survived an illness. Oh, how revoltingly smug can people be?

Don't they know they are really hurting grieving parents when they say that they believe their God decided my child wasn't worthy of living?

Under these people's understanding, they did something right and were 'graced by God', so by definition, I and/or my child weren't good enough to deserve his grace?

Oh, just piss off, you sanctimonious bastards!

If Brett's cancer and death was a punishment for some crime one of us committed, then it's a mistake because we are innocent. Kev and I only ever did good deeds and taught our children how to be good people. If it's because I didn't believe in the right God or speak to him in the right way then yes, I am guilty, but then, if such a god is cruel enough to punish my child for my crime, then fuck him anyway.

I cannot believe in a god that could save everyone but is selective and only saves a few. I don't believe in a god who could save the children from pain but who would choose not to.

However, the spiritual view is slightly softer. I guess I can believe in a god or great something of the universe where we are all individual souls who have come to this planet to 'play' at life. The spiritual view is more like we are souls who are part of the same wider consciousness who planned their game of life before they came down here. We chose what problems we wanted to face or experiences we wanted to have, although I have to question what on Earth I was thinking when I chose this game to play.

God would represent 'love' or 'the universe' rather than a parental, punisher figure. Souls who came to Earth and wanted to feel the good, the bad and the ugly experiences wouldn't need a god to save them, as it was all pre-planned in the first place.

I don't know what I believe, really – it all sounds a little bit like science-fiction. If our souls really left a beautiful, loving, safe haven, a glorious heaven, then aren't we all, in essence, crazy lunatics?

There's a quote in the Bible that says: "Blessed are those who mourn for they will be comforted." (Matthew 5:4)

I did a little research and I found it very interesting that the quote from Matthew 5:4 has a much deeper meaning than the initial face-value text. Blessed are those who mourn, for they will be comforted (I'm guessing by God), but the mourning as it's written isn't just meant exclusively for death; it refers to repenting of sins and acknowledgment of your own lack. The Spirit comforts those who are honest about their own sin and humble enough to ask for forgiveness and healing.

I'm not having a dig at the Bible here; for my part I only researched the quote because I saw it banded around everywhere whilst I was in my initial stages of grieving, just after Brett's death. It's quoted on sympathy cards, pillows, mugs and I saw a key ring of it online. The statement doesn't annoy me as much as the excessive use of it. A random quote from the Bible that doesn't even fully mean what it's supposed to mean to be thrown on merchandise – that's exactly what is wrong with society's attitude to death and grieving.

We hope that some invisible force will take care of our friends and family during difficult times as long as we're not called to step in and help.

They say, "Let go and definitely let God support you." (Anyone, just as long as it's not me because I hate sad, crying people, they're depressing.)

I do have to concede, however, that I think if people are honest and regardless of any religious attachments, people can sense that there is a reverence in death. From the midst of the despair during the time shortly before, and then after, Brett died, I think there was a strangely spiritual essence to the whole proceedings. I can't help but feel a connection to something that cannot be seen with the naked eye. There is a feeling of a power or a force around death that I cannot explain, but anyone who's felt it knows what I'm talking about. I can only conclude that there is a higher power, but that's as far as I will go.

Somewhere deep inside of me, somewhere in my consciousness, I do know my son has only gone back. He's gone home to where we all came from. Back to where we are all going to return to again. But he's very naughty and should have let me go first. Children shouldn't die before their parents.

I know I'll see him again and I know, strangely, that there's a part of my soul that is with him now. I often feel the presence of my son's soul, his spirit, and I know when he's around me, as it gets stronger in feeling, and the feeling is similar to a feeling of deep love.

Sometimes, and especially in the beginning after he'd died, the feeling would overwhelm me so much that the love would turn straight to sadness and tears. It still does sometimes now. But on a good day I can sit and just feel the love Brett and I share. There is a bond that his departure from the physical world can never break. I know a lot of people will think it's just wishful thinking, and maybe it is, maybe it's a fantasy that my subconscious mind has concocted to give me some comfort, but either way, I don't care. To feel the presence of my son's soul, his spirit, is a comfort, and I allow the feeling in whenever I can.

I have seen a few psychic mediums since Brett died, and a couple have been so good it's been breath-taking. It's been like actually talking to him. A really good medium can give you the characteristics of the person who's passed and information that no one else could know. I always cry when it's a really good medium because it's fantastic to actually hear from him and it validates my belief that he's around, especially when he can recount stories and has opinions about things that are going on in our life now. It reinforces my belief that he is somewhere, and if he is somewhere, then we will meet again.

There are bad mediums, so you have to be careful, and by careful, I mean don't give them lots of information, as they should be telling you, and especially don't act on their every word without question; you must continue to use your own head and logic. I don't think most of the mediums are 'bad' as such and I don't think they are just trying to steal your money. I think it's because they are often just given pictures, words or impressions from the spirit, and they have to decipher that it means. I think the so-called 'bad' mediums just need more practise, maybe? A good medium will ensure you don't need to say much and you won't be in any doubt whatsoever that they have connected to your deceased loved one.

It really annoys me that the shows on TV featuring mediums have to have a disclaimer saying 'the show is for entertainment purposes only'. I recently caught sight of the annual Easter church service on BBC One and I noticed that it didn't carry the same disclaimer. That will upset some people – the very idea of questioning a solid religion. The truth is, we don't know which religion is right and won't until we die.

I can imagine we go back to heaven (or wherever) after we die and have a life review. I'm sure I will be sitting there cringing at some of the mistakes I've made along the way, but I've never been a horrible person, up until recently. There have been times (and there sometimes still are) when I am so low and sad that my bitterness overwhelms me, and I think dreadfully mean thoughts and act out of character.

So, I guess I can't even claim I'm practising spirituality as my religion at present.

Love and light, maybe on a good day, but other times it's mostly pus and venom.

Namaste, bitches!

I should have a warning sign: "Danger! Grieving and godless." I wish I still believed in God; I do miss him.

I think we all know good from bad and right from wrong, I think we all know not to hurt each other and that we should be kind and try to help one another. I think most people are generous and equally know that love and happiness are the best emotions to feel. I think we all know how wrong we feel inside when we are being mean and nasty. We can self-judge and correct; we don't need a celestial referee keeping score.

Mass religion appears to be on the decline and scientists just love disproving anything with the slightest religious overtone; in fact, they seem to revel in it. The sad part is, OK, a lot of what is written in religious books seems unrealistic, but by disproving the existence of many religious figures and poking holes in the different religious theories, scientists have managed to take away something without giving anything back. Which just goes to make this cold and superficial world seem a little bit worse.

I will not know the truth about God until I die. Then, if he does exist, I hope he has a real good sense of humour and does not hold grudges! But I feel the need to warn him that I do.

With regards to religions and beliefs, my attitude is, do what you want to do and believe in what and whom you want to believe in. Whatever gives you comfort and makes you feel happy, loved and safe. Which is what I genuinely wish for the whole wide world... but only on a good day!

Chapter 7

The Kryptonite That Is Anger

I know a lot of people who went straight into a fury when their loved ones passed away. For me, my anger started way before Brett passed; it started during his long illness. This is a diary excerpt nearly three years into Brett's treatment.

8th August 2011

I'm frantically trying to research on the internet Brett's sensitivity to chemo, medications, steroids, etc.

Do we end treatment early, as suggested by the doctor today? Or do we try and struggle on? What if we end the treatment early and the cancer comes back? *But*, on the other hand, can Brett's body take any more of this torture? He is so ill, we are virtually living in hospital constantly whilst they firefight all the symptoms he has. The blood transfusions, the endless electrolyte deficiencies. He hasn't had a day free from pain since he was diagnosed in September 2008.

Enough is enough, maybe? But what if the doctor is wrong? He knows books and protocols and case studies, but on the other hand I know my child and he is so ill.

I'm busy researching across the world for any instances or cases such as Brett's and all I can see is a report of English people rioting. My son had desperately wanted to start work at the apprenticeship; we have just had to turn it down because of his health, and these evil, lazy little pricks are burning cars, looting shops and destroying businesses. Those spoilt, entitled brats are just behaving criminally and immorally because they can and will – they'll probably just get away with it scot-free. I am raging. Those little bastards are healthy, they have the health that Brett so desperately needs, and what are they doing with it? They are using it to destroy things and steal.

I wish them death, I wish them cancer, I wish them every little vile thing Brett has had to endure plus more. I wish one was in front of me now because I would literally beat them to death with my bare hands.

It's not fair.

Why should these scroats of society be allowed to live whilst all those beautiful, lovely kids struggle and fight for their very lives?

I hear the local teenage cancer ward has been hailed with bricks by the rioters. Vile little bastards.

I wish them hell, but unlike those of us who are living in hell, they actually do deserve it.

***

I was so grateful for Brett's wonderful initial team of doctors, and their staff, who seemed so knowledgeable and determined to help Brett fight and succeed against his cancer. Everything ran like clockwork; everyone seemed purposeful. They all had an air of confidence in both themselves and their colleagues that was infectious, and hospital life ran smoothly and, more importantly, calmly.

By the time he died, I saw the doctors and staff from both the hospitals that we frequented regularly (who had now changed 'teams' hundreds of times) as the enemy.

I witnessed cover-ups, abuse, lies, neglect, falsifying evidence and mistakes by the hundred. It was such a vile experience. In the last year of his life I felt at war with the hospital and staff. I had to be constantly on high alert for the endless stream of errors.

After Brett's bone marrow transplant and when he had no immune system at all, he had an antibiotic-resistant urine infection that was missed for a week. Two different samples had been taken and the results from the lab – in bright red: "Alert! Danger!" – were clear as day on the computer, but no one checked the results.

Brett ended up in intensive care with acute septicaemia and wasn't supposed to last the night, but he did.

He was in a dreadful state and paralysed from the neck down, but he was alive. I saw the doctors' faces, and 'What do we do now?' was written all over them.

The hospital carried on trying to look after him, but he still had no cells from his transplant. 'How was he even alive!' was the outcome of his mortality and morbidity conference that took place after he died.

Staff argued about how to care for him. Mistakes were everywhere. Physios that insisted on exercising his legs one morning, before the doctors had been round, physically lifted him out of bed to the standing position, only to watch every blood vessel in his legs pop just under the surface of the skin. Obviously panicking, they quickly put him back on the bed and frantically left the room, leaving me to explain and calmly try to tell him, whilst not letting him panic, that his legs were bright purple.

Bastards! Wimpy bastards! Turns out Brett had zero platelets, which is why all his blood vessels popped. "Sorry," they mumbled when we saw them again, which wasn't till the day after it happened. Doctors came from all over the hospital to have a look. Brett was more like a zoo exhibit than a human being.

Then came the doctors that didn't work on his case but changed the treatment. Weekend doctors would ruin the good work that the weekday doctors had achieved. I spent my life arguing.

Due to the septicaemia, Brett had terrible oedema, which is fluid retention that had caused his whole body to swell up like a large, painful balloon. The doctors had used medication to try and remove the fluid but without much luck, and the medication can damage organs (as can any medication) if used for too long. The consultant and her doctor worked hard to balance Brett's electrolytes with the belief that once they were all in their right place, the body would simply release the fluid quite calmly and naturally. It had taken a couple of weeks of daily grind for the doctors – upping this vitamin here, infusion of a little something else there – and suddenly, one Friday, it started working.

The urine the children passed had to be collected and measured by the staff and analysed against fluid intake to ensure there was enough going through and protecting the kidneys, etc., which was especially important during chemo.

This Friday evening the young doctor came running in with absolute delight that the plan was finally working and Brett's output was much larger than his input. She said it would probably continue over the weekend and she would see Brett on Monday, although there would be a lot less of him as he was happily going to pee the massive excess of water out. She virtually skipped off with glee at herself and the fact the theory had worked so well. The next evening, the Saturday doctor came into Brett's room. I had never seen her before, but that was the norm at the weekends. I sometimes wondered if they were just cleaners who had put a stethoscope around their necks. No, that's not fair… some of the cleaners would have performed far better.

The doctor promptly announced that she was starting Brett on a fluid drip. I laughed initially, thinking she was teasing, because he had been doing so well. But no, she was serious; as far as she was concerned Brett had lost too much fluid.

"That's the whole idea," I had argued. "Have you even read his notes?" was my normal frustrated weekend cry, but alas, no – she was adamant she was going to replace the fluids he had lost if he passed any more urine before midnight, which was the daily cut-off time. It was 6pm in the evening – of course he was going to pass more urine.

But he didn't in the end, according to their charts, because I put each of the subsequent urines down the toilet to ensure they weren't measured. Sunday, we just placed two out of three urines to be measured as we simply couldn't trust the staff team that weekend.

When Monday finally came and I recounted the story the doctors, they were furious, and this was one of the many reasons why I was allowed to request the consultants be called at home if I was unhappy with any decisions made at the weekend, or evenings. But I am just a mum and that pressure was so heavy.

The normal medication used to release fluid was called furosemide and it was given to any child on the ward that, upon balancing their fluid charts, was seen to have not passed enough fluid. It was to protect the kidneys, etc. It was a very regular part of hospital life and when it was given, you knew that child was going to spend the next four to six hours of their life virtually peeing. The last year of Brett's life, the 'team' insisted on giving it after midnight – why? I had no idea. When they could have done it every midday!

Some of the nurses would openly be laughing as they came in to give it the children. This ensured that the child and their resident parent weren't going to sleep at all that night. When I questioned lots of different staff members over the issue, all I could get was this standard response that it was protocol, but it hadn't always been, as I knew! Because I had been going there for five years. It was just another needless element that still now makes me furious – those poor children.

Then there was the battle of where to put him. Staff would try and move us out of the safe single room. Brett still needed isolation, as he still had no immunity cells at all, but staff would openly argue with each other, in front of us, about where to put him.

One night a decision was made to put him on a general ward which had measles patients in; it would have killed him. Kev had to run around the hospital trying to find any staff who were allies, who could back up Brett's need for the single room. Again, it was atrocious.

One weekend doctor came in and sneezed in his room, straight into the air, no hand up or anything, and just laughed. We looked at each other and Brett said to him, "I have no immune system."

The doctor replied, "Don't be silly. Of course you have, you haven't had a transplant… have you? I haven't looked at your notes." I later asked for him to be officially reported for his conduct. I doubt if the nurses did, as they sat at the nurses' desk giggling with the doctor for the entire afternoon.

The errors in medication were enough to make your hair stand on end. Brett used to check his own medication and regularly the hospital staff would give him the wrong doses. It was decidedly unfunny; in fact, it was frightening.

There were far, far more stories than this; what we lived through was simply atrocious and barbaric.

I believe categorically that in the midst of all this horrendous chaos, it led Brett to lose his zest, he was always such a happy upbeat person. He became so tired of the hospital, and the ridiculous and sometimes nasty staff, the conflicting opinions and rules, the disgusting food, the arguments, the drugs and painful procedures, etc.

This is why I think that anger wasn't a massive part of my initial grieving, instead exhaustion was.

For the first time in his life, Brett felt down and we were not surprised. Looking back, I'm not shocked that he finally went into slow multi-organ failure. His happy go lucky vibrant spirit couldn't survive the life he was having to endure. If only I could have taken him out of the hospital he might be here today, and that is the subject of the reoccurring nightmare I have. In my dream Brett is alive and thriving at home and we are simply ignoring the calls and hiding from the visits from the hospital teams.

They were more the enemy at the end, than the cancer was at the start.

I actually did write a complete book all about Brett's journey, and recently I took the decision to delete it. I kept diaries all the way through his treatment.

I decided I didn't want some poor family whose child had just been diagnosed with cancer to read our story. It was too hideous!

Had I known at the start what we had been facing during the next five years, I actually might have contemplated a mass family suicide; it would have been kinder to Brett without a doubt. I couldn't let people read our experiences; they need ignorance on their side. It would have been too cruel.

People often ask me why I didn't sue the hospital. I wrote multiple complaint letters whilst we were actually *in* the hospital, so after he passed, I wrote to the head of the hospital. I received eight pages of crap with a lot of 'sorry's on them.

Sorry wouldn't bring him back nor wipe away the disgraceful memories.

People talk about suing and wanting to be able to tell the world the story, but it's rarely allowed to happen like that. I found out most people who sue and gain compensation have to sign a gagging order preventing them being able to share the story with the world. I wanted the choice to speak or not. The hospital wasn't going to get a chance to tell me what to do ever again.

So, I decided not to sue. I wanted to escape the bastards, but if I sued them, I would have still been attached to them, probably for years.

And ultimately, I didn't actually want their blood money; how revolting to have their money in my hands where Brett's hand should still be.

Whilst our loved ones are alive but sick in hospital,

we mostly just get on with it. We are too busy living it and just coping. When the person dies and we have time to reflect, then oh, boy, you realise just what you've been through, and sadly, what you didn't need to go through. For me, there is no feeling worse than reliving those things you didn't need to go through.

I have very close members of my family who are nurses, and many family members work in the NHS. So please believe me when I say, I am not blindly bashing the wonderful work the mass majority of those staff do, day in, day out. But when there are toxic, nasty members of staff discovered, they must be got rid of. They infect the amazing good that all the other staff do. The NHS must learn to cut the cancer out of its own organisation.

I was working in a job I really enjoyed when Brett was taken ill in 2008. I struggled to give it up and it took me a year to admit that I wasn't going to be able to work, even part time, and be able to care for Brett. His side effects and conditions meant he was very poorly most of the time and I had to help him with washing and dressing. Obviously I also had the cooking and cleaning, but those chores weren't as important as the role of being there with him, trying to constantly 'cheer him up'.

He used to get very fed up and scared, although he would rarely admit it to anyone on the outside. Leukaemia has such a long road to go down, before you even finish chemotherapy. It's very intensive chemotherapy the first year, then a further two more years of lesser chemotherapy, which is to keep your bone marrow cancer cell-free. After that, treatment is stopped and the waiting game starts to see if it comes back. Brett's came back after ten months.

It was ten glorious months of health and happiness. It was like an oasis in a desert of pain and suffering. He didn't actually have a full ten months because he was still so ill when treatment halted; it took quite a while for all the drugs side effects to lesson off so he could have a normal-ish life. I would say six months, but wow, we all enjoyed those months so much.

If I had really known what he was going to go through when the cancer relapsed, that he would have to have the two transplants, become paralysed after a missed infection and die after being in isolation for thirteen months, I'd like to think I would have let him go at the relapse stage, but the truth is, I don't know.

Some days I think yes, I would let him go. Some days I would let him go right at the start in 2008, and some days, I admit I am selfish and would have him here now in any old state. I was good at looking after him and I loved his company. That's a sad admission, really, isn't it? Well, thankfully, I didn't know the future and the choice wasn't mine.

Strange, the things that bug you when someone dies, isn't it? After Brett passed away, the local family doctor came out to our home to pronounce him dead. The doctor said that his cause of death would be liver failure followed closely by kidney failure and then the bone marrow transplant. I said no, I wanted leukaemia as his cause of death.

The doctor was puzzled and looked at the notes that were on our kitchen table which had been left by the palliative care nurse. As he was reading, I said, "I don't want them to be able to use him as a success statistic. After all, he was cancer-free thirteen months post-bone marrow transplant, yet he still didn't have cells that functioned even after an additional top-up transplant. The hospital doctors missed an antibiotic-resistant urine infection that was reported on their computer system after *two* samples came back infected, over a week apart, and that error lead to Brett, who had no immune system whatsoever, ending up in intensive care with acute septicaemia. He wasn't supposed to last the night.

"Against the odds he survived, only to be left paralysed from the neck down. He learnt to walk again and coped with very painful neuropathy (nerve ending problems) and terrible oedema (fluid everywhere!).

"He struggled on for another six months in hospital until they conducted a liver biopsy through his *neck*, because they couldn't go in the normal way, as the infection risk was too huge, and then decided he would need a liver transplant and then another bone marrow transplant if he lived. Yes, OK, he was leukaemia-free, but would you call it a success, Doctor?"

I collected the completed death certificate a few days later room the local doctor's office. Who says doctors don't listen?

A few months after Brett died, and after Jamie's inquest (story to follow), I was very keen on revenge with regards to the awful things that had happened to Brett which really were totally avoidable, human errors, but I ultimately needed to find a way to continue living on this Earth, for my daughter's sake, and not become a serial killer.

By then, I was so full of anger that I could have literally walked into one of the hospitals that had treated Brett for his cancer and have shot some of the staff. I actually fantasised about it often. Hate was my fire and I knew it was going to destroy me if I didn't do something to cool the flames.

I hadn't felt angry initially when Brett passed. I think I was too exhausted; I simply felt an overwhelming sense of sadness tinged with relief. Relief that he was out of pain and 'the bastards couldn't hurt him anymore'. (Bastards being the medical staff.)

I didn't feel anything else. I was totally numb and dazed.

But when anger finally arrived, it was obvious that it wasn't going to go away again anytime soon. I was not just angry that Brett died; I was, and still am, angry about how much he suffered needlessly.

I can't forgive the hospital and staff that made him suffer more than he needed to. Some staff were brilliant, absolute angels on Earth. They managed to make a bad situation liveable; they were cheery, funny and kind. We all know these types of staff members; they can't do enough for you and the patient's comfort is their priority.

Then there were some staff – well, let's just say they needed shooting.

What was it all about, anyway? Over five years of pain and for what? All those awful side effects from Brett's treatment – him vomiting a minimum of eight times a day, diarrhoea ten times a day, his mouth, tongue and throat with the skin literally melted away, just leaving open sores. The fact that he was eating 3,500 calories per day and was still losing at least 3lbs per week. How his body was unable to absorb nutrients from his food; he was so thin there were bones sticking out of him that I never knew existed – he looked like a Belson victim. Also, I would have liked the doctors to have agreed with me to stop just one of his many chemotherapies that I believed was causing the most damage (I had noticed the pattern of increased illness during the four-weekly cycle over the three years he'd been given the chemo), but they wouldn't because they 'hadn't seen his side effects before'.

FYI, and to my absolute disgust, the chemotherapy that damaged Brett so badly is no longer given for three years' treatment! Instead it's only given for the first year now, because of its 'many nasty side effects'.

When I found this out, I felt simultaneously happily vindicated and equally furious.

I had been through so much over that one chemo; they had even threatened to put Brett into care. The doctors said they could take him away from me if it was seen as if I wasn't 'acting in his best interests'.

I eventually had to have a stand-up row with two consultants, during which I refused that chemo treatment and risked having Brett taken away from me. I could see what it was doing to him, even if they wouldn't acknowledge it. All this whilst receiving phone calls at 10:30pm on any random evening instructing us to come into hospital immediately because another vitamin or mineral was so low in his bloodstream it was risking his life, i.e. could cause seizures or the heart wall collapsing, etc.

The whole situation was nearly as much of a mess as my poor son was. I eventually won and the chemo wasn't given, but I believe, ultimately, that it was too late and the damage had already been done.

You can't make any plans during a long-term sickness. You don't even know for sure if you're going to watch a TV programme together that evening until you're sat down watching it. It's exhausting. I spend my life on high alert.

When I see on the news that parents of a sick child aren't allowed take their child and leave the country to seek different/better treatment elsewhere, it makes me so angry. In the UK we would still like to think we are world leaders in our fields of health, but I simply don't think that's true anymore. I think we're good, but we're definitely not always the best.

How arrogant do you have to be to let children die without allowing their parents the chance to at least try another course of treatment in a different country?

Well, about as arrogant as the table full of doctors who decide that those parents have no rights over their own child. It really twangs on my 'that's so unfair' nerve.

I really wonder if all the people out there in the 'normal, non-hospital' world realise just how much their children aren't *their* children?

They can be taken away in a heartbeat whenever our controlling nanny state decides to.

I get so pissed off when children with cancer are represented as little bald-headed angels with the sweetest of faces and big grins.

It's total bullshit; the reality should be shown instead. The screaming and crying, the deaths. They may sometimes be sweet and have big grins, but I can assure you it's not very often. You have to walk the corridors of a child cancer unit for a few hours to really appreciate the suffering, the crying and screaming these 'sweet little angels' go through. I'll never forget those child and teenage cancer wards.

As you left one of the teenage wards Brett was on, it led directly to the children's and babies' cancer ward. You had to actually walk through the whole length of their ward to get outside. It mostly felt very claustrophobic, but it was sometimes nice to see some other little faces, especially when they were all happy and playing, which sadly wasn't very often. More often than not there was just a general sound of crying coming from the wards. I used to try and walk as fast as I could to get out. I can still hear the noises now, years later. I think it taints the soul, hearing all those children suffering. (I really do feel for the staff for that reason.)

This one day I was walking through the child ward and I was aware of the ward staff walking around swiftly, obviously looking for a particular child, with a mother calling loudly across the ward for her. I had seen the little girl on a window ledge up by the teenage ward; it wasn't dangerous, as the windows didn't open, but the ledge and sides made a good place to hide for a little child and was often used as a fun hide-and-seek place. The little one was sitting looking very sad, and when she saw me walking towards her, she had put a finger to her lips, secretly asking, "Sshh, please don't tell them where I am."

I never gave her hiding place away, as I knew they probably wanted to do something horrid and no doubt painful to her. All in the name of beating cancer, and they would have found her quickly enough without me, as she had no place to go. The wards were like prisons.

I've seen so many beautiful children die and after such painful, intrusive, vile treatments. My God, these kids really do suffer. And I am so tired of pretending it's OK. These brave cancer kids often die after years of misery. It is not a pretty nor a fun existence for them. If the child is old enough, they get completely robbed of their own peace of mind, and not only do they have to face the death of the other children around them but they also have to face their own mortality and spend time discussing what happens when they die.

Desperate parents, who very often have turned their backs on their own religions, struggle to discuss some of life's biggest questions, with their own very sick children.

Spending all those years in the hospital system, experiencing all the errors and mistakes, has left me feeling very angry and worried. I was previously blissfully unaware of the sheer volume and extent of the human errors that occur in our hospitals. The vast majority of staff were kind and generally responsible, but there were some that were purposefully mean, and some who seemed quite stupid.

You simply didn't expect nasty staff members in a children's hospital, but they certainly existed.

If I ever recount one of the many horrible events we experienced during Brett's treatment, somebody will often say, "Oh, don't worry, karma will fuck them up," but I don't think I believe in karma.

If I believe in karma, then I have to believe Brett's illness was a punishment for wrongdoings to him, me or our family, and I can categorically assure the world – we did *nothing* wrong.

I don't think even karma could be that evil.

Brett's cancer was a harrowing insight into all things dark and evil. I learnt things I had never wished to learn and saw things that can never be unseen.

From the minute you're given that cancer diagnosis, you and your family's freedom has ceased to exist. You are now the sole property of the hospital that will be dealing with you, or hospitals if there are multiple ones, like we had. You also lose your child and your family as a 'unit' on the day of cancer diagnosis, but you just don't realise it until much later.

You have every element of your life dictated to and there's no arguing. They choose if, and when, you may leave the city to spend a day at the seaside (for us that was twice in five years). They decide if you're going to have family birthdays or Christmas together (heads up, you're not going to be able to have any special days – well, not as you knew them) and if you dare argue, they will threaten to take your child away from you into care.

If you're not going to play the game their way and abide by their rules, they will go to court, quoting that you're 'not acting in the child's best interest'.

So, you begin to feel as though if the cancer doesn't get your child, or the harsh treatments, the hospital system will.

It was hard for me to relinquish control of my family to a faceless hospital system. I really struggled with having doctors, consultants, specialist nurses, cancer social workers, dieticians, physiotherapist and occupational therapists, etc., all asking intrusive questions about my private family life and having to make amendments to suit their particular criteria. Especially when very often their 'advice' actually contradicted their colleagues.

Upon diagnosis, you enter a scary and unfriendly goldfish bowl. Dignity, choices and family decisions are out. You are owned by the system, the very system that has been set up to save your child's life, so you should be grateful, and most of the time I was. Extremely grateful, especially when you consider the fact that in the UK we don't have to pay for our medical treatment.

Maybe in hindsight it was karma, because it often did feel like we were all being punished. The wards were secured better than a young offender's unit; in fact, young offenders had a far better social life than the majority of teenagers with cancer. If you nipped off the ward to buy a drink or grab a breath of fresh air, one of our particular wards needed entry by two different alarmed doors, which were only allowed to be opened by staff. It sometimes took an age to get back into the hellhole; allegedly it was for our safety, but it certainly didn't feel that way – to keep people out, they locked us in.

Even now, the whole thing – the dark memories and awful times we endured, for no apparent reason – makes my blood boil with rage. Come on, karma, do your thing.

The Day That Anger Came to Stay

On one rainy April day in 2014, I attended a coroner's inquest of a lovely boy who had been in hospital with Brett. He had had his bone marrow transplant a few months before Brett and he had also died, which wasn't particularly surprising, as the cancer kids were dropping like flies around us. What was surprising was that although most of the parents around us, including us, could reel off the mistakes the hospital was making with their children, we couldn't really prove the mistakes, whereas these parents could.

Jamie Cartwright had died of aspergillus, a lung condition caused by dust. Now prior to the children having their bone marrow transplant, hospital staff actually come out and inspect your home to see that it's up to standard. They check its clean, mould-free and in a good enough condition for the child to come home post-transplant (not straight away, but many weeks after when it seems like the transplant has taken hold and the cells are growing well). During the time prior to the transplant, it is drummed into you that you must 'not even put a nail in the wall' for fear of the dust and, in particular, contracting this very lung condition. The Cartwright family had followed the rules to the letter, but sadly the hospital itself had not.

There had been building work going on outside the hospital for months. Dust used to fly everywhere, the noise was deafening and the corridors were filthy. The builders used to cut the concrete slabs with mechanical machinery just outside the exit from the cancer ward. I myself used to be frightened, and when Brett was in his wheelchair we used to stay inside the corridor in the hospital and wait, watching for a time when we could run (literally running with his wheelchair), avoiding the plumes of dust. Brett used to cover his mouth with his coat, as we knew how dangerous the dust was. Whilst we were on the hospital wards some parents had complained about the ongoing building work and we had been given letters by the hospital reassuring us that everything was fine, totally safe, in line with health and safety guidelines, and we were not worry.

The only reason I was attended the inquest was because I had been contacted by another grieving mum, asking on behalf of the Cartwrights, did I by any piece of luck still have that original letter? I went through some of Brett's paperwork and there the letter was. I took it to the coroner's office the morning of the inquest and handed it to the Cartwrights' barrister. The hospital was denying ever sending the letter, so now I was intrigued and decided to stay and watch the inquest along with another grieving cancer family. I'm not sure if it was a good idea in hindsight, as that day changed my life. I watched in horror as person after person from the hospital lied under oath.

"No, there weren't any skips outside the hospital," they repeatedly said.

What? my mind screamed. *That's an absolute lie.*

"No, there wasn't any dust at all," they all individually pledged when questioned under oath.

That's a total lie – how can they lie? I thought.

"The building work was safe and followed strict guidelines," they answered.

During the inquest it was eventually admitted that the hospital hadn't even got the basic health and safety policy guidelines in place needed to do the building work on a normal home, let alone a hospital specialising in treating rare cases and seriously ill children. By the afternoon the hospital had made itself look horribly inept and literally deadly inefficient, and the Cartwrights had been vindicated. The coroner's verdict was that the hospital was at fault for causing Jamie's death. The Cartwrights had won the inquest – although it was no win, as lovely little Jamie was still dead.

The worst thing for me was watching them, including our own doctor, lie under oath on the stand and seemingly so easily. I wanted to scream, "For God's sake, we all walked past the very big, open skips daily and you're saying they didn't exist!"

My blood seemed to freeze inside of me when it eventually dawned on me that if they could lie to a coroner and court under oath so easily, could they have lied to me about Brett?

My heart started beating loudly; it had felt like it was going to burst out of my chest. I progressively got angrier and angrier as the day went on, and the anger has never completely left me since.

From that day forward I never spoke to another member of the hospital staff again; I just couldn't trust them. The inquest had opened a wound in me that would never heal. I couldn't trust myself either. I mentally reviewed and re-reviewed conversations and meetings with Brett's doctors – had they covered up too? Did they lie to me? Oh no! If only I'd known how untrustworthy they were sooner. I was so tired too when Brett died, so maybe I didn't fight the doctors enough – maybe I didn't do enough? Maybe I trusted them when I shouldn't have? Along with so many other unanswered questions I have, I'll never know.

So where does that leave me now? It leaves me the bitter, twisted, angry woman I swore I'd never be. The spotlighting ability of anger in grief is like a magnifying glass to an ant on a sunny day.

I often feel I hate the world and everyone in it. I sometimes just want to attack, and I am so disassociated from the rest of the world. I think they're all a bunch of idiots. And why do normal people moan so much? Why do they moan when they have absolutely nothing to moan about, yet they drone on incessantly about... Crap – pointless, trivial crap. No one cares – is that all you have to worry about? You silly arse!

The grief and the anger take any small cracks that existed before in relationships and turn them into grand canyons, but we were lucky, as we had experienced all that angst during Brett's illness. In his death we had unity.

You know those people who love drama, sympathy and just generally need any attention, and we all know some of those people right? I often wonder why they didn't get my life. They would have loved it; they could have really revelled in the disgusting spotlight we were in. They would have had a reason for people's sympathy forever, whereas in contrast I am a very private person and I hate attention or any fuss-making, and I loathe and detest people feeling sorry for me.

People can be really patronising too. Kev was off work due to the stress of Brett's illness. I think at this particular time Brett had tried to 'die again' and had been in the ICU with a bad infection. Upon returning to work, Kev was made to go and see the company's occupational therapist. Kev was forced to tell this therapist all the gory details, why he had been absent from work and why Brett had been in the ICU again, etc.

She had sat and thought for a moment and then said she understood completely what Kev was going through, as it was just like when her daughter had broken her leg.

Kev had sat in silence waiting for the therapist to tell him the part where her daughter's life was threatened, maybe because she had been operated on and ended up in the ICU, but no, as the story went on it transpired that it was, in fact, a very normal, standard leg break – no operating theatre, no ICU, no hospital admittance at all.

But this stupid woman thought her experience was on a par with us and our life.

After Brett died, Kev had struggled, as he worked on a factory track assembly line which made engines, so his work was repetitive and monotonous. He wasn't sure he could continue because he didn't really care if the engines got made or not. His managers would come and shout at the staff to work quicker and harder, and he would just think, *It's a stupid piece of metal, who cares?* He eventually took voluntary redundancy and left.

You can't help but analyse your life and wonder about the sheer futility of it all, why you're doing the things you do and if you still care or not. The truth is, nothing matters, really.

People around me have said they feel cheated because since the death I've changed. I say, "Oh, cry me a river!" My anger is triggered by all the unfairness in the world, and there is a lot of it, so I'm pretty much angry all the time. Anything that appears unjust, unfair or just not right, and I'm on it, exploding like a firework.

Bad customer service, being ripped off, bad quality food, grumpy receptionists. Oh my God, if you hate your job, then resign.

I'm not happy the way I am, but it just is what it is. I can't really relax in public and be normal anymore, as I have to watch myself a bit because sometimes my behaviour has shocked even me.

One summer after Brett has passed, I was walking the dogs in a park when I saw a family – mum, dad and two children – out having a picnic. The mum was angry at the children and was shouting and swearing so loudly at them that they looked utterly terrified. The husband just looked a bit embarrassed and generally confused, so he obviously didn't know why she was so angry either. It was all I could do not to go over and slap her. I felt so incensed at her behaviour – didn't she know how precious those children were, how quickly the time goes and that they could even die? I stood shaking my head at her; we locked eyes and I could tell she knew what she was doing was wrong. She put her head down and silently packed the picnic away whilst her husband hurried the children off to the playground. I just stood and continued to stare at her; my mind was saying to me that I should walk away, but I couldn't move. I was fixed to the spot; I really wanted to go over and hit her. She had everything I used to have, yet she wasn't happy. *The stupid cow, I'd thought.* I eventually managed to turn and walked away, but I'm sure by that time I was probably scaring the woman a bit. She never looked up at me again, but I knew she knew I was there.

I look at some bad parents and think to the universe, *Why take my child? I adore my children – these bastards wouldn't even care if their children went.* It's a terrible thought, and I am inundated with ones just like them.

I was driving along after Brett had passed away when a horrible gang of young boys walked slowly straight out into the road a little way in front of my car. They were staring and smiling at me arrogantly as if to say, "We know you'll have to slow down because you won't hit us."

In an instant I slammed my foot on the accelerator and I sped up. They moved quickly enough – the startled looks on their faces was very satisfying indeed – but in that spilt second, I realised I wouldn't have cared if I had hit them.

In that moment my head had screamed, *My son is dead and you vile little shits are left on this Earth instead! What a fucking joke.*

There's a quote from Buddha which says: "You will not be punished for your anger, but you will be punished by your anger."

I don't know. I disagree – I think it will very much depend on what mood I'm in at the time to see exactly who's going to get hurt.

Chapter 8

Life Goes On – Bazinga!

When someone you love dies, life goes on around you just the same as at it did before they died, and I feel it's one of the worst aspects of it all.

I wanted the world outside of me to reflect my world within. I wanted the whole world in mourning and laughter banned, music cancelled, joy outlawed and the sky to be covered by foreboding black clouds.

I remember the spring after Brett died, I was driving Poppy to school, when the sun came out from behind some clouds and shone through the windows into the car. I thought I might spontaneously combust when the rays started warming my skin. How very dare the sun! I didn't want to be warmed; the shining sun was repulsive and offensive to me.

I don't want Brett to be some fading memory, but I fear that that's the reality to the people around me. What was initially deemed as shocking, appalling and unacceptable, has become quietly accepted by them.

Time doesn't heal the real wounds of losing someone whom you truly love. Loss cannot be quantified and assumed to be hurting less simply due to the passing of minutes and hours; that's merely the ticking of the hands of a clock.

What difference does the length of time actually supposed to make? None whatsoever for me since losing Brett. Although, time seems to have a shape-shifting ability depending on how I feel in that particular moment, thereby making Brett's passing appear to alternate between feeling like forever or just five minutes ago.

There seems to be such a small time limit allowed for grieving, imposed by those who don't or maybe can't understand. I don't know if their lack of compassion and thought is due to never having experienced a close loss or just the fact that they're idiots who are too caught up with posting selfies of their breakfasts!

What even is grief, anyway? One overused word with a million feelings attached to it.

In my opinion, you're not the sufferer of grief but instead you're the sufferer of love, and I hate hearing this, "Don't get stuck in grieving, see a doctor if you're got complicated grief."

I am not stuck in grieving my child – I am stuck in the sheer, pure and immense love I have for him, so I guess I'm stuck in love? OK then.

And 'complicated grief', which is a relatively new pigeonhole for people who don't fit in to any of the experts' other pigeonholes.

For me, the constant referencing to this nonsense belief that grieving someone is something that you can expect to just quietly go and gently dissipate away is very misleading. You falsely wait for the sadness to go, and on some days when you feel good, you think, *That's it then, grieving all over*, only for an event or memory during the next day (or hour) to trigger you and you're on the floor in agony again.

I've accepted that I can't cry enough tears to be done; it's never going to be over. Not that I've cried too excessively, tears seem to be the tip of emotional iceberg anyway, but those little bastards keep escaping from my eyes, even when they are not welcome nor convenient.

It's really frustrating that I can't find anything physical to do to show how much I miss Brett and how sad we are that he's not here.

I light candles every night to show I'm leaving a light on for him, that he's loved and missed and thought of, but I want to do more; it never feels enough.

The little word 'grief' cannot explain the existence of the array of feelings that goes into the loss of someone you adore.

I was doing the ironing one day; it was less than a year after Brett had died. I noticed with some horror that my yellow T-shirt had a hole in it. The hole was right in the middle of the T-shirt at the front, so I couldn't wear the T-shirt, as the hole would be too obvious. I switched off the iron and suddenly became nearly hysterical. I had worn that T-shirt for years. It was a pre-cancer life T-shirt. It had been there through all the cancer appointments, the surgeries, the time spent living in hospital. I had hugged Brett in that T-shirt many times and now it was going to have to go. My husband came into the kitchen and asked what had got me so upset. I explained, through teary gasps of breath. He simply told me to keep the T-shirt, but I knew there was no point, as it was just the first of many things that Brett had seen or touched that would disappear over time. I threw it in the bin, still crying; the little yellow T-shirt represented him going and our life having to continue without him.

Our possessions have been subconsciously divided into pre-Brett's death and post-Brett's death, with the pre-Brett's death items being priceless to us.

You try and get back to being the same as you were before he got sick and died. But the old versions of us don't exist anymore, so to go back is impossible. You have to find a completely new way of being, of coping or merely surviving. We as a family had to find a new life and a new way to be; the past way was too painful for us. We moved house, opened a business, wrote a couple of books and I am totally comforted by the knowledge that we are living a life that we simply would not have been living if Brett had survived. Attitudes, beliefs and values have all shifted and changed too.

The exposed hurt and pain has changed me so much that I feel as though there appears to be a rip in my soul; I cannot stand any suffering. I feel everything so acutely now; I am so raw. Humans, animals, bugs – I cannot watch anything that shows them suffering. Spiders get gently placed outside. Kev saved a bumblebee the other day. It was a hot day and the bee was walking down a path seeming unwell and was going to get stood on, so Kev picked it up with some card and placed it under a bush so it was in the shade and cooler.

Recently it was one of the cancer children's heavenly eighteenth birthday. Happy eighteenth, Jay! Can you imagine a world where his mum and I would spend well over an hour on the phone on his actual eighteenth, talking about all the dead children? I mean, it's just so sad, but that's the reality when your child has died. I do get great comfort talking to another mum who 'gets it'.

Ultimately the outside world needs to understand, I don't need therapy and I don't want solving. I don't need saving, but noticing my loss now and again would be nice. Let me talk about my child, my baby (who died at eighteen and would now be twenty-five years old). Let me tell stories and share memories, help me keep him present even though he's gone; that's the only soothing thing that actually works, albeit in a tiny way.

***

5th December 2017 – *Not the Most Wonderful Time of the Year!*

I grabbed a few things from the supermarket and I was on my way home. As I exited the supermarket, thirty carol singers seemed to scowl at me in unison as I tried to ignore their high-pitched singing and precariously placed donation buckets, and just left the store as quickly as I could. Just as I finally got past the group, one of the carol singers said something about 'so much for charity' to the woman next to her and they both laughed. It was obviously about me. I was going to go back and give her a piece of my mind, but what was the point? Nothing would change the Christmas cheer mafia: "It's Christmas, be happy or else."

I wanted to scream at her that my child died at Christmas, and every little piece and part of Christmas – like the carols, the tinsel, the mince pies – makes me want to throw up. Not everyone can be happy, and a lot of people suffer more because it's Christmas. It's actually the most unsympathetic time of the year.

Christmas for me is a time of agony. I feel like a war veteran with PTSD who is sent back out to do another tour of duty whilst the rest of the world around me parties.

Why is avoiding Christmas not an option? Why can't one supermarket per town be allocated to not have Christmas items at all? Why can't I wear a badge that shows an upside-down Christmas tree as a sign to the happy, clappy prats around me that I don't celebrate Christmas and no, actually, I don't have to be happy, merry nor bright?

From late August I noticed Christmas cards being sneaked into one end of an aisle at my local supermarket. *You've seriously got to be kidding me*, I thought, and was disgusted as the children hadn't even gone back to school.

Then, in September, as the Halloween aisle got into full swing, I noticed more and more Christmas items being put alongside the initial Christmas card offering.

The day after Halloween was over, Christmas had sprung all over the store. *Oh my God, it's really coming*, I thought to myself as the cold, awful feeling of dread filled my body.

Christmas is a living hell for us. The tinsel, the carols, the sickly-sweet family adverts that advertisers spew out, all remind me of that awful time when Brett died and what's missing from my life now, or rather, who's missing.

We were told in hospital on 23rd December 2013 that there was nothing more they could do for Brett. His final wish was to die at home, so it was swiftly organised. He was to travel home on Christmas Eve for the last time.

Whilst being transported home in the ambulance, it seemed as though every Christmas song known to man was belting out of the radio. The songs like 'Driving Home for Christmas' and 'Have Yourself a Merry Little Christmas' had never felt so cruel and acid-like before.

Poppy had been told earlier that day that her brother was dying, ensuring that not only would she be forever heartbroken but her view of Christmas would be ruined too.

The last Christmas we had enjoyed as a family was in 2011. Brett was free from cancer and we were excited and so hopeful for the future. Christmas 2012 was spent in strict isolation during his bone marrow transplant in a children hospital and obviously Christmas 2013 will always remain the worst.

Even when the children were small, I never really bought into the whole big Christmas thing. Of course, there were presents and nice food, but we were always quite broke. My husband worked in a factory and I was a stay-at-home mum. I was determined I wouldn't get into debt for Christmas.

I didn't think bankrupting ourselves was the true meaning of Christmas, and I know it's a cliché, but those cheap Christmases were the best because we were so happy and we were together. The food shopping wasn't much more than a normal weekly shop; after all, Christmas dinner is just a Sunday roast and shouldn't cost the Earth, so extras, maybe like a pack of biscuits or some crisps and fizzy pop, would be added. The children got nice presents, but only what we could afford. The house was cleaned for Christmas, but I never bought new furniture or decorated especially. 'Order now and get it in time for Christmas' is a marketing ploy used by every retailer in the country. I think it sort of sweeps people up and along, but considering Christmas is supposed to be a time of peace, goodwill and joy to the world, have you ever stopped and looked at the faces of the people in the shops? They are the polar opposite.

Normally it's miserable faces, elbows in your sides and the battle of the car park space.

The cancer families who also lost their children understand, and it is a sad comfort to be able to talk to other parents of children who've died of cancer, as we are all members of the very worst club in the world. We can share just how hard it is to continue in life generally and especially at times like Christmas without one of our children. Not surprisingly, I hate and despise Christmas now.

I never wanted to hate Christmas; in fact, I used to adore it. The happiest time of the year, snuggling in the cold winter's nights under blankets watching Christmas feel-good movies, which have to have a happy ending – it's Christmas law. Presents under the tree, Christmas carols blaring out; my house was so over-decorated that it looked like a cheap and tacky Santa's grotto. There was such a thing as overdoing it and I overdid!

Peace and goodwill to all except to the miserable bastards who couldn't even smile, which, rather ironically, is now me. I am that miserable bastard who scurries around shops and town centres avoiding merriment at every possible turn. I just want to get back to my safe haven, my home with no sniff of Christmas anywhere near it. I slam the door behind me after every hurried excursion out in the dreaded month, breathing a huge sigh of relief to be back safe and sound and free to be sad in my home that looks no different on 25th December as it does on 25th June.

I had to leave a trolley full of shopping in a supermarket and just walk out the first year after Brett died, as the song 'Driving Home for Christmas' came blaring out in the store and I didn't know if I was going to throw up or faint. I learnt to wear earphones and play my own music whilst shopping (Eminem is a favourite).

People don't understand, though. "Be happy, it's what Brett would have wanted. Brett loved Christmas." I know he did. We all loved Christmas when he was alive – well, except for the Christmas that he slowly died over, or don't you all remember that one?

Oh, how quickly they forget. People send me cards without my son's name in them. What crazy mindset does that? Don't you wish my dead son a Merry Christmas even if he is in heaven? It's just so thoughtless. People also don't invite you anywhere, thankfully. Who'd want a family of downers at their Christmas parties? It's just as well that we're not invited, as I'd only say no thank you anyway. I need my space to be miserable. It's my choice; it's what I want.

I do not have the energy to fake being happy at the very time of year that is my total misery, my very reason for despair.

And what can I say to the Grim Reaper, my arch-enemy, my nemesis; you chose Christmas to deal your final blow – how heinously cold and cruel.

Christmas is just pain and heartache to me and my family, but I am not naive enough to think we're the only ones. Christmas to thousands of people is a sad and lonely time. If you've lost loved ones the pain is heightened by the constant stream of 'happy family' images being thrust down our throats at every opportunity by the advertisers, whose only aim is to make us spend, spend, spend. Anyway, people should be warned, one day I might snap and stick that bucket from the moaning carol singers just where the sun don't shine.

Chapter 9

Death Day – Funeral Day – Happy Birthday

The hardest times of the year for most bereaved people are supposed to be special occasions. I find this nonsense; any day can be hard. Ironically, I'm writing this chapter a few days before my son's birthday. But his birthday comes just after the anniversary of his death and the day after his funeral.

Today is the anniversary of when I last saw his body in his coffin, dressed and ready to go.

I put his birthday cards and other bits in his coffin to go with him, I made sure he was comfortable and warm in his new coat – totally illogical yet equally necessary.

It wasn't him, by the way. It didn't really even resemble him – well, maybe vaguely. He looked like a waxwork doll version of himself, devoid of any lifelike features or comparisons. He felt pretty much cold and yucky physically to touch, which, ironically, is just how I felt inside on the emotional level, along with distraught, devastated with a dazed, pain-riddled feeling of shock.

Tomorrow is the anniversary of his funeral and wake, and then the day after that is his birthday. Blimey, it couldn't have been planned worse if we'd tried. It's all a bit much, really, but you have to play the cards you've been dealt, I suppose.

I find his birthday the most frustrating of all the anniversaries because I still want to do the usual. I want to do what I've always done; I want to celebrate and spoil him.

My brain still runs the old programs of: *Got to get Brett's presents, must buy a cake, get a card, are we having a party? Should I buy party food anyway, because he always changes his mind from no fuss, please, to yes, let's party. What day is his birthday on? Weeknight, so we will need to do something nice yet low key on the actual birthday night, then have the party at the closest weekend. Must go shopping for his gifts, what shall I get him?*

That speech is literally just off the top of my head. The tapes run constantly; they are obviously automatic, but then, when my logical voice interrupts those tapes with, *Hey, he's dead!*, I get to feel a deep pang of sadness and grief, over and over again.

It's like I have an internal automated self-harming mechanism that I can't switch off.

At random times of the year I will see something in a shop and think, *Oh, Brett would love that!* And I will have forgotten in that moment that he's dead. Sometimes, though, I still buy the item and put it in his room or the cabinet I have for all the 'Brett things' I have bought in his memory.

But more often than not, the sad stab I will have felt from remembering he's gone will have prompted me to move away quickly and get on with whatever I was doing in the first place.

I wish I didn't have to go through the pain of having a day, such as a birthday, with no birthday boy. I always end up trying to imagine what we would be doing now if he wasn't gone. Such fantasies only tend to lead me to frustration and anger, accompanied by deep sighs and wine bottle opening. (Such days allow the question, "Is it six o'clock yet?" To which my husband always answers, "Somewhere in the world.")

Equally, though, sometimes the anniversaries do allow love to be poured back to you, especially via social media. Brett's Facebook page is still active, and it is a source of real comfort when I see his friends posting nice comments and expressing their appreciation for him.

I always feel like a version of Sally Fields with her infamous Oscars speech; I sit with my phone in my hand reading his Facebook messages smiling and saying, "They love him, they really love him."

Brett's first birthday without him was the day after the funeral and was nothing but a cold blur.

On the second birthday after Brett's death, I decided to get Brett presents, things I would have normally got him, and I wrapped them up and put them in a pile next to his box of ashes.

The day of his birthday came and I realised, with some horror, that I would have to either open the presents myself, get someone else to do it or throw them away unopened. What had I been thinking? How stupid of me.

I opened the presents and put the stuff I'd bought him on shelves in our living room, which grew the shrine to him that had already started. Friends and family would buy things they thought he would like and put them on the shelves. The shelves grew into a cabinet and now we have two cabinets.

We will always get Brett cards and put them up on the mantelpiece, and I do try and buy one thing for his birthday, just because it makes me feel a bit better. If I didn't do that, I'd worry that he's watching me and saying to himself, "Oh, cheers, Mum, not bothering with me already?" And I know as I admit that thought and write it down, it looks so stupid and illogical, but it's nonetheless how I feel.

This year we've decided to have a Chinese meal for Brett's birthday meal. We also have Christmas crackers (ironic, really, as we don't celebrate Christmas anymore). It's a silly tradition – we always did have Christmas crackers at his birthday. They were normally being sold off in the supermarkets cheap and Brett, when he was small, would say, "Can I have these for my party?" Who says no to a little birthday boy?

Poppy's at college in the day and it's the first year we're not all together all day on his birthday. I don't mind; Poppy loves college and it's important she's allowed to not feel obligated to do anything rigidly on the anniversary days. After all, she misses him every day, not just one day a year; she lives with the grief as well.

People talk a lot about the first anniversaries and say they're the worst. I disagree. Sorry, I think they are all bad. People make a lot of effort in the first year, which slowly drifts off as time goes by.

Who decided one, two or three years is long enough for the need to put any effort in?

It's not as if three years on the friends and families look around at each other quizzically and say, "Who died again? No, I don't remember that person at all." I guess they see no need to do anything to remember him.

Within the grieving cancer families' group, honouring the special sad days has become so difficult, as we have all done everything we can think of: let off balloons, let off butterflies, let off doves, names in the sky, names in the sand, names carved in stones and gold, ashes and fingerprints and their handwriting in jewellery, there's tattoos and portraits, there's trees and flowers and plants and plaques, and benches and charities all in memory of our beautiful children who passed.

I was talking to another mum the other day and we really think we're done – whatever next? But there is a real deep desperation that we all share, and that's to keep our child's memory alive.

Sometimes I'm not even entirely sure it's just that. I

love trying to plan things in his honour and just saying his name. Oh, my! That feels so good. Brett, Brett, Brett.

On my darker days I feel like the anniversary days are just for people to show the world, and the dead, that we've not forgotten them completely, a sort of one-day-only remembrance pay-off. "Here's some flowers, see you next year."

I get the impression sometimes that friends and family feel obligated to show that they care, I get vague 'thinking of you' texts, which is nice, much better than no texts at all. It's been six years and people wouldn't want to encourage me to wallow in grief, would they?

It's so stupid, though. I mean, how ludicrous to think I only think about my son on a few individual days a year. He literally is my first thought in the morning and my last thought at night. My house walls are adorned with large photos of him and always will be. There isn't a room in my house that doesn't have mementoes and reminders of him; even the bathroom has his shower gel and deodorant.

Very soon I'm sure the anniversary of death, his funeral, his birthday, will all be just small private affairs. I feel the world does move on fast and honouring our dead loved ones is a one-stop shop, a one-time-only event. "Funeral, tat tar, now let's move on."

I love my son; he lived, he actually lived, and took breaths and had hopes and dreams too. And his birthday, the very day he came into this world, will always be celebrated, and he resided here for eighteen long years. I wish he was here now, but wherever he is right now or wherever the energy or spirit or soul which is Brett is, he will know I am thinking of him and sending him all my love and squishy kisses.

Happy birthday, my beautiful son.

***

Because of Brett Facebook (there is also a 'Because of Brett book' Facebook page too)

This is an excerpt from our Facebook page which we started to celebrate Brett's life, on the day he passed away.

The 30th December is getting closer, and this year it marks six years since Brett passed away, and for some reason it's harder and sadder this year. So very sad.

So, this year and every year after, we want to try and remember Brett 'the person' and who he was, and I'm sure still is.

Brett loved life and people and laughter. He was generous to a fault and would give anyone his last £1. He loved sport and to gamble; he loved shopping and designer goods. He loved a good money-saving deal and a good price. He loved a good joke and most music.

He just adored people and loved more than anyone I know.

He lived many lives in his short time and tried to cram in as many experiences as possible.

So, this year we want people to do something awesome Because of Brett.

Not because Brett died, but because he once lived.

He lived, he loved, he laughed, he partied, he gambled, he kissed, he joked and he spent money.

So, on the 30th December, do something BECAUSE OF BRETT. Maybe buy yourself or someone you love something nice, place a bet or buy a scratch card. Anything luxurious, as Brett loved luxury, so maybe a nice bath as it doesn't have to cost money. Maybe watch your favourite box set or film. Just something that spoils you or someone else.

Because Brett would have spoiled you. Brett loved life, and he would love this idea, ha ha.

If you want to, you can post what you did here, as we would love to see.

So, remember 30/12

Because of Brett xxxx

We have recently added something new to the Facebook page.

We have had silicone bracelets made that are sky blue, of course, which is Brett's football team's colour. And they have on them written in white: "Because of Brett. Impossible? Do it anyway."

The idea is that people take the bracelets with them or simply wear them when they travel or go somewhere nice and take a picture with the bracelet and then post it on the Because of Brett Facebook page.

For me, it is literally people taking a physical reminder of Brett with them, I love the (my) idea so much and I adore seeing the pictures immensely. Brett would love the attention too, as he wasn't exactly a shy man. Friends and family have really got behind the idea, and we have had some lovely photos in very interesting places.

So brilliant, and thank you, everyone, it means so much.

Chapter 10

My Way – Lovely Jubbly

Death is probably the scariest, darkest thing that happens in our society all day, every day, yet it's the least talked about. Outrageously stupid when you think that it's the one thing, the single solitary event that we all have in common.

We are all going to die, and so are all the people we love and cherish most dearly. Yet we have no 'lessons' on death when we are growing up, nor do we really talk about it with other adults. We try and ignore death, and pretend it's not going to happen.

We avoid people who are grieving, instinctively knowing it will be us one day. If ever there was a huge elephant in the room, it's death.

Spike Milligan, the British comedian and writer,

summed it all up with his famous quote (which I later found out was actually a Woody Allen quote): "I don't mind dying. I just don't want to be there when it happens."

There's never a good time to die, as the people around you are never ready. It's always a bit of a general inconvenience too. My husband's mother died when Brett was in the middle of his ten months' remission from cancer. Some would say that was great timing; others would say not so much.

But I guess the real question is, how do we lose someone we love and adore without losing ourselves in the process?

Before Brett got ill, I had tons of friends and a very close family circle. I was the type of person who would help you out in a heartbeat and I would be there in your hour of need, no problem. I would stay on the phone for hours if a friend was sad or upset; I put myself out for people all the time, to the point where it drove my husband mad. But I thought that's what you did for each other and I suppose I expected the same in return.

I was destined to be sad and extremely disappointed. Now, I am very wary about getting close to new people because you never know a good friend until you need them, and by then it's too late. I'm hugely suspicious of people and I'm not very trusting at all; I'm probably damaged and too punch-drunk from the effects of life.

Some people seemed to think I was just going to pick up my life where I left off, almost as if that whole 'Brett thing' had been just a blip. "Gee, I'm glad that's over now, where was I… oh, yes, I had a career, a social life, friends, money and unbroken heart, and a sense of humour."

The fact of the matter is, I couldn't come back even if I wanted to. The person I was before Brett's illness and death is dead herself; she no longer exists. I'm not trying to be melodramatic, but I've seen things no one should see, and I've experienced and continue to live with pain I never thought imaginable, so there is no picking my life back up.

I now see life for the shallow existence it can be. Full of shitty, fair weather friends. Whilst life is great, we're great, but when life gets sticky, it's, "Bye-bye, call me when things are better."

Being around people who understand, such as another family grieving their child, is a feeling like you're home, yet it's the worst club in the world to be a member of.

There's such guilt at living for parents of children who've passed away. Our children so desperately fought and simply wanted a chance to live. It's hard then, because if you don't live some sort of life, you are kind of wasting your life, which must in some way insult them in heaven. There's no way to win, it feels. The only way for me to live on was for him.

Life is so fragile. The good news is the pain caused by the death of our loved ones is temporary and loss is not forever, as we eventually all die too. The saddest thing is that the deceased are nearly always ready to go, but we who are to be left behind, are not ready for their departure.

Grief is the sadness and disappointment that we just wanted the chance to still share time with our loved ones, and to travel along this Earth together, and when someone goes home first, and dies, we feel a bit cheated and alone. You can never cry enough tears to be done. There is no moving on; the road is closed and there are no diversion signs.

Death is natural and inevitable, and what isn't natural is to expect everything to always remain the same, yet death often twigs on our 'it isn't fair' nerve.

I think whilst viewing the world around us, the meaning of grieving may have gotten lost in translation somewhere. Rather than spend a little time remembering and honouring our lost loved ones, we instead are supposed to hurriedly grieve and move on. I wish people would try to soothe the bereaved more, rather than eradicate, downplay or dispel our feelings.

Whereas I say to people grieving, "Do whatever the hell you want."

Be as individual in grief as you are in life. Maybe grieving is even the wrong word; maybe it's 'honouring' them instead.

I shall live in 'honour' of Brett; I am 'honouring' my son every day, but I guess it still highlights the missing and that bloody empty chair.

I think overall, it's simply better to accept the brokenness of it all, and the pain, because I feel it's unavoidable. At the end of the day, grief is only an expression of love.

I say, put that loved one in your pocket and take them

everywhere with you. Talk to them, include them, never let them go – if that appeals to you (although I really, desperately, don't want to appear like I'm ramming my opinions down anyone's throat, because the bereaved are all too familiar with people around them doing that.)

When grieving, I think it's best not to wait for better days to come, because you'll wait forever; today is your life.

When you look at it coldly, the world seems to care deeply about pointless things and just generally, as Brett would say, "Chats shit" (which is to talk incessant nonsense). Grief's insights do give you lightness with regard to the rest of the world; the lightness is the realisation that you see through all the facades, the fake and the plastic. Death makes status become irrelevant.

I don't care what people think. I couldn't give a toss about people's opinion or advice. which is more often than not a case of 'you take my advice because I'm not using it'; it often seems like the blind leading the blind.

My grief is summarised by the fact that I struggle to function the same as I did in the past. I struggle to sing, to dance, to breathe and to just 'be' in this world where Brett is not. I talk all the time to my boy. I ask Brett if he's not busy to come and see me (like you would a normal child). All the time I look for signs and feelings that he's around.

Brett is my joy, so I enjoy keeping him with me and his memory alive.

You don't need to be a psychic medium to know something other than this world exists; we all instinctively know. But even if our departed loved ones are with us in this new type of relationship, it's not a very satisfying relationship. We can't have our tea together, have a good gossip, then go shopping.

I miss his hugs. The hurt never changes and the sadness never goes; there's a void inside of you that nothing fills. Grief is like a living entity inside of you that growls at everything and everyone around you.

I light candles every night to show I'm always thinking of him, leaving a light on for him, and he's loved, missed and thought of.

Some days I am in a good mood and some days I'm a mess.

Some days you can have a nice, friendly chat with me and some days I want to bitch-slap everyone I meet, and yes, I still reserve the right to fall apart at any time in the future if I want to.

As I've previously mentioned, prior to Bretts illness I was a professional life coach, which you probably won't believe after reading this book (with all its expletives, spewing venom and so forth), I was a pretty good one too. I was optimistic, positive, smiley, action-planned, powerful and just all-round brimming with glorious yumminess.

I'm no longer a life coach, and for a while I actually deeply despised and resented the 'rah, rah' crap that spills from these self-appointed 'you can do it' gurus.

When you're caring for your son who has cancer, the bubbly 'there's nothing you can't do' brigade made me want to say a heartfelt and almighty, "Oh, do me a favour and just fuck off."

There's a physical dent in the wall of my home where I got so enraged at a book that was about death. The book seemed smarmy, smug and self-righteous; it was all about the positive aspects to someone dying: "Death is just a journey, maybe one that helps the living reframe their lives…" Bang, against the wall it went.

Maybe it actually did help me? I had thrown the book with the greatest velocity across the entire length of the room; it had smacked at great speed off the wall (hence the dent) then I went over, picked the book back up and proceeded to rip it apart whilst screaming loudly. The energy I expelled during that outburst made me feel so much better – once I'd thrown away all the pieces of the discarded literary bollocks.

I've heard it said that the soul doesn't grieve. I guess it doesn't need to, because it is that part of us that knows the truth about it all. It doesn't wonder, worry nor torment itself with 'what if's and 'should of', 'would of', 'could of'. It's cool; it knows.

My mind doesn't just talk; it plays songs (on repeat), plays films, role-plays scenarios (normally very sad) and it has impressive, full-blown arguments, normally playing the part of multiple angry characters simultaneously.

I think that is why a lot of people gain respite from the grieving process when they can shut off the chatter from the incessant talking mind. Maybe the soul is the calmness behind all the noise?

Have you ever heard an iPod when is nearly empty? A little voice comes on and says, "Low battery, please connect to power." It made me think, *I wonder what our human power source is?* Love, maybe? How do we connect to power? I don't know.

I used to think it was alcohol, as it had always worked for me in the past (I am English, after all), but now, maybe it's meditating, I think, or generally *not thinking*, as in just quietening the mind.

Don't get me wrong, shutting the mind off and sitting quietly with the soul doesn't make you happy; it's not a cure for sadness (there isn't one). But mindfulness and meditation definitely help me. Although the mind isn't the only problem, because the body grieves too. Those aches, pains and illnesses you have are real but equally no doubt caused by grief too.

There's a quote I love, and I apologise because I can't find who first said it, but it's: "I meditate, I do yoga and I still want to kill someone."

Yep, that's me. I am angry at the world at large and at my little piece of it. I was angry at the people around me, that they didn't help more and that they didn't do enough.

But the truth can be more painful than lies. The people around me didn't let me down, as they could never take the pain away. And, to be brutally honest, I didn't want them to, because for a while, pain was all I had left to show that Brett had existed.

We are all strong enough to cope with death of a loved one. You can, and will, get through it. As a cancer mum, I know how strong and resilient we all are. For some reason we are fed this constant stream of rubbish that we are not strong enough, that we are somehow weak and need fixing. It's all bullshit.

I saw some of the biggest of life's fuck-ups (some of the other parents). I'm talking about some really weak, selfish and stupid people, who stepped up to the plate in those cancer wards, and they all did impressively well, without exception.

We're not broken or inadequate; when the challenge comes, you cope, and no one said it had to be pretty (I can vouch for that one). Cry all the way through the funeral or vomit outside the chapel if needs be; never move on and just do what you need to do. It hurts, but it doesn't kill you (or make you stronger either – that's just more bullshit too). Grief is sometimes a case of learning how to be who you've now become. You're changed – be kind to yourself.

Great strength doesn't come because you've experienced a dark, sinister world; it comes in spite of it.

So how do we live on without our beautiful, special loved ones? For a start, as basic as it is, we live on because they want us to. They've reluctantly had to tag out of the game, but they're still watching and egging us on, supporting us from afar. They never gave up, so we mustn't either.

Remember, we are all still together, just not physically. We need to stop with the 'they're dead, just move on' game; instead we need to talk about them and end the silence.

Let's have decent conversations about our dead loved ones, whether they are young or old, human or animal;

was it death by illness, accident, suicide or by the hands of another?

Let's share and talk more:

What did they do here on Earth that mattered to them?

How did their lives make a difference to the world, even if it was in a tiny way?

Did they love you? Of course they did; then they absolutely changed the world, even if it was just your world, for the better.

I think they want us to talk about them, to honour them, to show that their life touched us, that their character was special, and how they were funny, loving, kind and special. I think they can feel our love for them when we express it, instead of hiding it away.

I know Brett is everywhere. He is the feeling of pure love and appreciation, and all that's good in the world. He exists in that feeling when you see a beautiful summer sky or a sunset; he is the delight you feel upon hearing a beautiful chorus of birds or a stunning piece of music; he is in the sound of the sea crashing onto the shore; he is the feeling you have when you get the promotion or your team wins. The love we share is in everything and anything that's joyous or wonderful. (Better stop now, as I wouldn't want you to throw the book at a wall.)

Let's honour our dead loved ones, remember them, talk about them and show them that their life mattered. Show that you remember their smile and how they made you feel. Did they make you feel special, loved, clever, adored, worthy? Then that's their legacy to you. What do you remember? What touched your heart? How did they impact your life?

With a lot of the cancer kids, I remember their laughs and smiles, the fun times. How they made it easier to get through those horrible days together and there was real camaraderie between us all.

Without exception the children and teenagers with cancer, whom I was lucky enough to meet, were some of the nicest, kindest and most interesting individuals I've ever met. They were special people (and their families too), and it was an honour to spend time with them. They had unbelievable courage and grace, and they taught me more about the human spirit than anyone else has ever been able to.

They all touched my heart, and their legacy for me when I think of them (which is very often) is just how humbled I feel I am to have known them. They say you shouldn't meet your heroes, but I met lots of them in those wards. They were so special. I really do hope we all meet again on the other side, and I can imagine as I cross over to the spirit world that someone will meet me by shooting me with a nerf gun (as they did on those wards).

Brett's legacy for me is massive.

He had such generosity; he was very creative; he inspired me. He acted 'today', and it was always 'now', not tomorrow. He had a wild sense of adventure and fun in his spirit. He was extremely funny and had a very quick sense of humour. His eyes shone when he laughed, which was often. He was so loving; he was inclusive and everyone was his friend; he was forgiving and compassionate. He was one of the good guys, and I am very proud to be able to call him my son.

This was one of Brett's favourite quotes:

"Life is not measured by the number of breaths
you take but by the number of moments that
take your breath away."

I wish everyone who reads this love and peace, and please reach out to me on Facebook at 'Because of Brett the Book' and tell me about your lost loved ones.

*"Bring out your dead and I will bring
out mine, our loves will never die."*

Chapter 11

Somewhere Only We Know – My Ramblings to Brett

People ask me how I am. How do they think I am, Brett? I've lost a most beautiful part of my life and I'm supposed to be 'over it' by now. How do I get over you? People watch you grieve like it's a spectator sport. The dead turn into faceless blobs over time and our collective society allows and even encourages it. People cringe if I say your name; their eyes widen in fear if I start telling a story about you, and not a moment after the final syllable will have left my lips will the subject be swiftly changed over-eagerly by a nearby companion, much to the relief from those around me.

Bollocks to them, is what I say. I'd like to see them cope. You're not a faceless blob; you are my son, my best friend, a character in the story of my life, and not just any character – no, you are a major player, a main event. You, along with Poppy, are my life. I hate, hate, hate the fact I have to use past tense when I reference you. You *were* a good lad, you *were* funny, and surely you still are? Surely you're funny and loving and kind and sweet *now*, wherever you are.

Are you really OK, son? Are you warm or cold? Do you eat or are you hungry or don't you need food? Do you cry for us? Are you sad too? Do you long for us to die and be with you? Are you lonely?

Do you need me? Did I do enough, enough to try and save you? Do you hate me and think I'm a bad mum? Was it your time or did that hospital cock-up (well, the string of cock-ups, actually) kill you? Could I have saved you? Could you have been saved? What would have happened then? Would you have ever been healthy or would you have spent your life in hospitals and in pain? Do you remember the pain you went through? Can you still feel it? Did you really suffer in vain? Why? Why did it all happen?

What was it all for?

Is there a God? Are you with God now? And does he know how very mad I am with him? Does he know I hate him? People say I should rejoice in the fact God gave you to me in the first place, but I think it's easy for them to say; they haven't had to give their child back so soon. Or maybe they're just better people than me.

Did I do something wrong and that's why God punished me by taking you? God couldn't have hurt me more. He should have taken me instead; why didn't he take me? I had nearly triple the time on Earth that you had, and I hadn't suffered like you. If God knew all along that he was going to take you back, why did he put you through five years of pain and suffering? Why does God allow children to have cancer?

Did you forgive God?

Is there a heaven?

Are you happy? Do you have a home and somewhere nice to stay? Does someone look after you? Do you have friends? Have you met up with all your other cancer friends that died? Are they OK? Do they know just how much they are missed? Can you give them kisses from me? Do you see how stuck we all are? Can't go back and don't want to go forward. Don't want to go forward without you. It's too hard. It's too sad. We are too sad. Sad isn't a good enough word, but there isn't a good enough word to explain the depth of despair that I feel without you.

You were such fun and together, the four of us – well, we were going to conquer the world. The fun and laughter we shared could fill three lifetimes – do you remember all the fun? Do you remember going to the seaside on mad, spur-of-the-moment day trips? The arcades, the beach, the chips and ice cream, playing football whilst Poppy built sandcastles that you then knocked down and made her squeal.

Wherever we went you always bought a little metal toy car. You loved cars. Do you remember the traffic jams you used to build on the window ledges? I wish you could build them now. I've built one for you at the new house.

Do you still love cars? Are there cars in heaven? Do you have one? What colour is it?

Do you know that because of you I don't fear death, because that's when I will see you again? I will hold you so tight and you will tell me how cuddly I am and that you love our cuddles. I am very cuddly at the minute – well, just fat, really.

Do you see me? Can you see how fat I am? It's just that I don't care, really. I care about your dad and sister, of course, but nothing really matters, does it?

Did you see we have dogs now? They are lovely and you would have simply adored them. I wish we had had dogs when you were here. I wish we hadn't put lots of stuff off for tomorrow. I wish we had done more. Do the dogs see you? Do you visit our house and make our dogs behave funny? Are you what they are watching when they follow someone across the room when there's no one there? Is it you? I wish I could see you. I miss you.

They say that I shouldn't be sad and I should just think of you as going next door – well, if that was the case, I would just shout over the fence to you and you would shout back to me. Why us, Brett? Why our family? We never did anything wrong. We were lovely and just normal, quiet, nice people. I'm not very nice now – do you see me when I get mad? Do you see how bad my road rage is? Do you see how I walk past charity boxes and scowl at carol singers? You would tell me off if you were here, but you're not and that's why I'm so mad.

So very mad. The time's up for me now. It's been over six years, so we are supposed have gotten over you by now. We are supposed to have moved on with our lives.

Just crap, isn't it.

Do you see the people who tell me you would have wanted me to have moved on? Really, how do they know? What makes them so sure? They didn't know how close we were; they didn't know all the plans we had made together for in the future when you were better.

They don't know. They just think it's a good thing to say. But there isn't a good thing to say. They weren't there with us all; they don't know.

It will always be a time only we four know.

I will hold on to our memories tightly.

I will try and make you proud.

Until we meet again, my wonderful son.

We will forever live on together as a family of four, 'somewhere only we know'.